Coping with

bipolar

disorder

Coping with
bipolar
disorder

A CBT-informed guide to living with manic depression

Steven Jones

Peter Hayward

Dominic Lam

ONEWORLD

OXFORD

COPING WITH BIPOLAR DISORDER

A Oneworld Book

First published by Oneworld Publications, 2002
Reprinted 2003, 2004
First published in this new edition, 2009

© Steven Jones, Peter Hayward, Dominic Lam, 2002, 2009

ISBN 978–1–85168–699–5

Cover design by Mungo Designs
Typeset by Saxon Graphics Ltd, Derby, UK
Printed and bound in Great Britain by TJ International, Padstow

Oneworld Publications
185 Banbury Road
Oxford OX2 7AR
England
www.oneworld-publications.com

Mixed Sources
Product group from well-managed
forests and other controlled sources
www.fsc.org Cert no. SGS-COC-2482
© 1996 Forest Stewardship Council

Learn more about Oneworld. Join our mailing list to
find out about our latest titles and special offers at:

www.oneworld-publications.com

Contents

Series foreword

This series is intended to provide clear, accessible, and practical information to individuals with a wide range of psychological disorders, as well as to their friends, relatives and interested professionals. As the causes of emotional distress can be complex, books in this series are not designed purely to detail self-treatment information. Instead, each volume sets out to offer guidance on the relevant, evidence-based psychological approaches that are available for the particular condition under discussion. Where appropriate, suggestions are also given on how to apply particular aspects of those techniques that can be incorporated into self-help approaches. Equally important, readers are offered information on which forms of therapy are likely to be beneficial, enabling sufferers to make informed decisions about treatment options with their referring clinician.

Each book also considers aspects of the disorder that are likely to be relevant to each individual's experience of receiving treatment, including the therapeutic approaches of medical professionals, the nature of diagnosis, and the myths that might surround a particular disorder. General issues that can also affect a sufferer's quality of life, such as stigma, isolation, self-care and relationships are also covered in many of the volumes.

The books in this series are not intended to replace therapists, since many individuals will need a personal treatment programme from a qualified clinician. However, each title offers individually tailored strategies, devised by highly experienced practicing clinicians, predominantly based on the latest techniques of cognitive behavioural therapy, which have been shown to be extremely effective in changing the way sufferers think about themselves and their problems. In addition, titles also include a variety of practical features such as rating scales and diary sheets, helpful case studies drawn from real life, and a wide range of up-to-date resources including self-help groups, recommended reading, and useful websites. Consequently, each book provides the necessary materials for sufferers to become active participants in their own care, enabling constructive engagement with clinical professionals when needed and, when appropriate, to take independent action.

Dr Steven Jones
Series Editor

Acknowledgements

The primary inspiration for this book came through our clinical experience of working with people with a diagnosis of bipolar disorder and their relatives. We have also all been involved in clinical research into the effectiveness of psychological interventions for people with this diagnosis. We have found people with bipolar disorder to be a diverse and fascinating group whose resilience in the face of their often very substantial difficulties is humbling.

In our experience the efforts to cope of both people with bipolar disorder and those close to them are impeded by a lack of ready access to information relevant to their condition. It is therefore our hope that this book will go some way to providing people with bipolar disorder, and others who may be interested, with information on a range of issues relevant to their diagnosis as well as indicating the important role that people can play in their own treatment, both psychological and medical. Many people have offered help and advice with this manuscript, including Jenifer A. Bright, Mike Calver, Sophia Frangou, Tom Fahy, Clare Martin, Robin Forman and Carol Larkin. Their help has been invaluable and we hope that we have made good use of it. We are also very grateful to Katherine Taylor, who made many useful suggestions for improvement to this new edition.

Chapter 1

What is bipolar disorder?

Introduction

This book is intended to provide information for people who are experiencing bipolar disorder, along with their relatives, friends and other interested lay people. Bipolar disorder is the term that is now used to describe what was formerly known as manic depressive illness. The focus of this book will be on providing useful information about the nature of this illness and its treatment. This information will include both traditional treatment approaches and more recently developed psychological treatments. It is not the intention of this book to imply that people with illness should treat themselves, but rather that by having access to relevant information they can take an active and influential role in the course of their own treatment. As authors we have both clinical and research experience that attests to the usefulness of psychological approaches to bipolar disorder. We are also well aware that at present these are most effective when used in combination with more traditional forms of psychiatric treatment, in particular with appropriate forms of medication.

How common is it?

Bipolar disorder is not uncommon. Around 1–1.5% of the

population in both Britain and the United States are expected to be suffering from bipolar disorder at any time. This translates to around one in every hundred people having a form of bipolar disorder that would be recognised by psychiatrists. This figure alone indicates that a large number of people are living with bipolar disorder and this does not take account of milder forms of mood difficulties that would not be diagnosed as bipolar disorder but could still cause significant problems for those experiencing them. This includes cyclothymic disorder, in which the individual tends to experience relatively frequent changes of mood (both elevated and depressed) but in which no single episode is so severe as to require a clinical diagnosis of mania or depression.

Symptoms of bipolar disorder

It is important to note first that in the press and elsewhere there is at times confusion between bipolar disorder and other psychiatric disorders, such as schizophrenia or personality problems. In actual fact the symptoms that identify bipolar disorder are quite specific. Bipolar disorder is a severe form of mood disorder during the course of which a person experiences both extremes (low and high) of mood. Extreme low mood is diagnosed as depression. There are several different means by which a clinician can diagnose clinical depression, but all these means of diagnosis identify certain essential symptoms.

Depression is characterised by persistent low mood and loss of interest in previously valued activities. Sleep is often disturbed, as is weight, and both can either increase or decrease when someone is depressed. Feeling extremely tired is common as are feeling either very slowed down or very keyed up. People will commonly feel guilty for no good reason when depressed and tend to be extremely critical of themselves. Thinking can feel difficult and attending even to quite straightforward tasks can seem to be a great burden. Thoughts of ending life or of wishing no longer to be alive can also occur.

It should be emphasised that people with depression differ substantially. Just as people are individual in the absence of mood disorder, so they are when they experience psychological distress. Whilst one person may feel agitated, guilty and indecisive, someone else may feel exhausted, slowed down and constantly in need of sleep. These symptoms need also to be present for a significant period of time, at least a couple of weeks, so that someone feeling depressed for a day or two even if they felt very low would not normally be diagnosed with depression if the problem then resolved or significantly improved. Clearly, everyone experiences mood changes and experiencing a significantly low mood is a common experience. It is the severity, duration and extent of impact of symptoms that differentiates clinical depression from 'feeling depressed'. Following is an example of depression.

case | *Laverne currently suffers from depression. She is now forty-one years old. She had two episodes of mania in her early twenties, but none recently. Her main problem is that her mood is low and negative most of the time. She has raised her daughter alone, in spite of her mental health problems, and her daughter as a young adult is now attending college and doing well. Laverne is, however, very critical of herself. She sees herself as a failure and struggles to maintain employment as a cleaner. She thinks a lot about what she sees as her own shortcomings. She has described herself as 'Jonah, cursed by fate'.*

Mania is usually thought of as being the polar opposite of depression. However, this is not entirely accurate. Whilst some people with mania can indeed feel elated or very happy, it is not necessarily the case and irritability or short temperedness are common.

Common symptoms of mania include feeling oneself to be superior to others; this can be intellectually, physically, in appearance or in terms of specific talents. People during mania often need less sleep and sometimes might go for days at a time without sleeping. There is usually a tendency to be more talkative than usual and to speak more rapidly. The listener can therefore sometimes feel bombarded by the rate, volume and length of conversation of someone in a manic phase. Ideas will often seem to appear one on top of another, cascading out in speech that can then be hard to follow as the person with mania struggles to keep up with the rate of different and divergent thoughts that they want to express. Intense interest in work, hobbies or new projects may become apparent – working excessive hours without rest or sleep in following up a big idea. Because of the person's often high self-esteem during this phase there will be a tendency to continue putting effort into plans even when others reject and try to dissuade the person from engaging in them. The smallest element of praise can at this stage be interpreted as a ringing endorsement. When in a manic phase concentration can be poor because of easy distraction by other information, and there is also an increased danger of engaging in risk-taking activities. These might involve increases in sexual promiscuity, thrill seeking, drug or alcohol use. Often this pattern will be grossly outside the person's 'normal' character.

Again, this is a pattern that needs to be present at a severe level for a significant period of time (at least a week) before a clinical diagnosis of mania can be made. As with depression, there is great individual variation. Some people will seem to have some elements of the above symptoms as part of their 'normal' character and therefore the manic phase is merely an extreme variation on this pattern. However, for other people the manic phase will involve behaviour and actions that appear entirely foreign to them when the phase has passed. One person might therefore experience a manic phase in which mood is elated and they are carried away with a sense of their own inspiration and superiority, which feels initially very positive but becomes less so as acting in an impulsive manner starts to cause practical problems. Another person might experience mania as being associated with high, and therefore unpleasant, levels of irritability and agitation, in which talk is very rapid, many conflicting ideas are present at the same time and it is very hard to accomplish any tasks because of this combination of other symptoms. In the following example Donald exhibits psychotic symptoms.

case | *Donald is thirty-two and lives with his parents. He has been in hospital four times because of episodes of mania. The first occasion was as a student. Having been quite shy at home, he became more sociable and outgoing at university. He found his first girlfriend, started drinking and began to use cannabis. His mood became more expansive as the first year continued and he began to sleep less and less. He started to tell his friends that he was 'inspired' as a writer and had a great future. Over time both his writing and his speech became more rambling and incoherent and friends and family found him increasingly difficult to understand. He noticed that he had brilliant ideas that came into his head so fast that he couldn't follow them. Towards the end of his first year at university he was found wandering around the campus and talking incoherently. He was admitted to hospital at this point and treated with anti-psychotic medication and lithium.*

Psychotic symptoms can occur in either depressed or manic states. Psychotic symptoms are, essentially, unusual and false perceptions. The main psychotic symptoms that a person might experience are delusions or hallucinations. A delusion is a strongly held belief in something as a fact despite the clear presence of evidence indicating that it is not true. Hallucinations are the experiences of seeing, hearing, touching or smelling something when there is nothing there. Auditory hallucinations are commonly heard as voices speaking to the person. These voices may seem like a running commentary to the person, or the voices may be threatening. This can be distressing for some, but others live peacefully with their voices. Most common are auditory and then visual hallucinations. Here is an example of a delusional belief:

> case
>
> *In her early twenties Laverne was admitted to hospital twice with manic episodes: during these episodes she believed that spirits were possessing her (a delusional belief). She slept very little and would stay up late at night listening to music and finding 'spiritual' meanings in lyrics to pop songs.*

An additional feature of bipolar disorder is hypomania. People who experience hypomania will, as with mania, experience elevated mood, often increased self-esteem and greater sociability. Thoughts and speech may come more rapidly and risky behaviour (sexual, drug taking, or other stimulation seeking) may increase. It is different from mania in that there are no associated psychotic symptoms and changes in hypomania will be less severe. Many people have experienced brief periods of hypomania as a positive state in which they have been creative and productive. However, as it persists there are substantial risks of the state worsening into depression or a full mania, as the following example demonstrates.

> case
>
> *Melissa is twenty-eight years old and works in advertising. Her mood fluctuated in her teens and early twenties, generally between periods of low mood in winter and feeling energised, creative and sociable in summer. During one of these 'up' periods she ran up big debts on her credit cards. She allowed herself to be picked up by three men during this period and found herself involved in group sex. She found this degrading and upsetting and a period of low mood followed. Memories of this incident continued to trouble her for years after the event.*

Causes

Bipolar disorder has a history of being seen as a clear example of a biological form of mental illness, that is, a disorder in which there is a medical brain problem that is in need of medical treatment to return the person to health. As will be described in more detail below, there is evidence that bipolar disorder can be inherited and also that there are important biological factors involved in developing this disorder. However, it is also clear that the relationship between inheritance, biology and bipolar disorder is far from being a simple one. In fact, there is additional evidence that experiences that individuals have in their lives, how they respond to such experiences and their general patterns of thoughts, feelings and relationships are also important factors in whether or not bipolar disorder might develop. The possible role for each of these factors is discussed below.

Genetic

The first genetic evidence came from studies into the extent to which bipolar disorder (then known as manic depression) ran in families. It was found that although not everyone with this disorder had relatives with a similar illness, many people seemed to. Overall, estimates seemed to indicate that if a person had bipolar disorder, there was approximately a 13% chance of that person having a relative with depression and a 7% chance of him or her having a relative with bipolar disorder. However, it is worth considering that this also means that the chances of a person with bipolar disorder not having a relative with either disorder are vastly higher (87% and 93% respectively). Even when studies have been undertaken of twins who share identical genes (monozygotic twins), the chances of the second twin having bipolar disorder if the first did were not 100%. Around 67% of twin pairs who shared the same genes had bipolar disorder in both twins. This means that 33% of such twins did not share bipolar disorder in spite of being genetically identical.

Evidence to date does indicate that genes have a role in bipolar disorder. It is, however, also the case that many people with this diagnosis have no family history of this form of illness and, furthermore, many people with bipolar disorder go on to have children who are well. Therefore, the effects of genes on illness are complex and combine with many other different factors to determine whether or not a particular individual goes on to develop the illness itself. Recent information from the mapping of the human genome provided interesting evidence that the number of different genes in the human genome was much lower than that expected. Indeed, the figure reported was not substantially higher than that of lower mammals. This has been interpreted by geneticists as indicating that experiences after birth must have a greater impact in generating the diversity in human beings than had previously been supposed by scientists who were investigating primarily the biological and genetic elements of human functioning.

Organic

As bipolar disorder can involve many areas of human functioning, and also since there is evidence that drug treatments are effective for many people with bipolar disorder, a lot of research effort has gone into the investigation of possible abnormalities in brain function of people with bipolar disorder. Although there have been a number of studies that have seemed to show differences in brain chemistry between people with bipolar disorder and other groups, findings are not consistent. Also, there is at present insufficient evidence to link any one specific abnormality to the features of the disorder itself. For instance, the finding that the depressive phase of bipolar disorder is improved by medication, which increases the brain chemical serotonin, does not necessarily mean that reduced levels of the same chemical caused the original depression.

If brain differences are finally established, they will have to be consistent with the fluctuating patterns of bipolar disorder and take account of both extremes of mood evident in this illness. It is likely that any brain abnormalities (if present at all) will be found in the interactions between structures involved in integrating and organising different brain functions.

Environmental

If genes or biology were the only factors that influenced bipolar disorder, then the experiences a person has in life should not affect whether he or she develops the disorder or becomes ill again subsequently (relapses). However, there is clear evidence that in the period leading up to first becoming ill people will often have experienced significant changes or problems in their lives. The significance of these problems will usually be greater than those experienced by people who do not become ill. Once a person has received the initial diagnosis of bipolar disorder, further periods of ill health will again often be preceded by life events or difficulties in the period leading up to ill health recurring. In the past, there had been suggestions that this apparent relationship between people's experiences and their subsequent mood problems was misleading. It had been argued that this association just reflected the fact that people were beginning to become unwell and their behaviour was then responsible for causing difficulties in every day life. Researchers, working first in the area of depression and later looking at bipolar disorder have therefore distinguished between events that could be described as *dependent* (caused *by* the person) and those that are *independent* (not under the control of the individual). An example might serve to illustrate this distinction:

If a person lost his or her job in the weeks leading up to an episode of illness, then this would be a *dependent* event if it were the result of the person's increasingly erratic behaviour. However, it would be an *independent* event if it followed satisfactory job performance and the firm the person worked for was in the process of reducing its workforce for economic reasons.

When this distinction is made and researchers have looked at how many independent life events occur prior to a period of illness, they do seem to be more frequent than in periods of good health for an individual, or for comparison groups who do not become ill. Therefore, the experiences people have do appear to have a potential impact on their mental health and this cannot be solely explained by a person's own behaviour being affected by the early stages of illness.

Personality

There is no single type of person who develops bipolar disorder. However, there are certainly a number of people with high levels of motivation towards achievement and significant levels of perfectionism who suffer from bipolar disorder. Of course, there are also many people with the same characteristics who remain psychologically well. People with a history of fluctuating mood, variable enthusiasms and periods of despondency are said to have a cyclothymic personality. There is evidence that people with this type of personality are at increased risk of going on to develop bipolar disorder. However, it should again be made clear that many people who go on to develop this disorder will not have had such a personality prior to its onset.

Course of illness

Age of onset

Bipolar disorder seems usually to be first diagnosed when the person affected is in the later teenage or early adult years. One major review of age of onset suggested that the highest risk period is in people between fifteen and twenty-four years. This is an illness that often begins in early adulthood, although it can occur at any stage of adult life.

What can cause episodes of illness?

There are numerous possible causes for episodes of illness. As noted above, the experiences a person has can be associated with periods of either depression or mania. These can be positive or negative experiences, but are characterised by having a significant level of impact on the person's functioning. Thus, the birth of a child might generally be regarded as a positive event, but sometimes the associated strain of changing roles, lack of sleep and possible additional financial burdens could be associated with increasing levels of stress. This could in due course be associated with illness in someone with a sensitivity to bipolar disorder.

It seems that people with bipolar disorder can if anything become more sensitive to such experiences as they get older. Poor sleep, alcohol and drug use, and erratic work and social routines are all possible factors in the occurrence and reappearance of bipolar symptoms. Our research and clinical experience indicates that individuals with a diagnosis of bipolar disorder can identify experiences that might cause them health problems and can develop skills to avoid such situations. When avoidance is either not possible or not appropriate, then people can learn to take steps to protect themselves at an early stage from the consequences of such situations.

Social and personal costs of bipolar disorder

In the past, there was a tendency to describe bipolar disorder in relatively benign terms. There was an assumption that although specific episodes of depression or mania could be severe, they were also time-limited. Furthermore, and in contrast to views about schizophrenia for instance, it was assumed that people were actually quite well in between the episodes that brought them to the attention of psychiatric services.

More recent work has, however, indicated that although some people do indeed cope very well with their lives for the vast majority of the time, there are a lot of people who have to cope with significant levels of symptoms even when they are 'well'. That is, many people do not have sufficient symptoms to be said to be clinically depressed or manic but may at the same time have combinations of symptoms that serve to make day-to-day life very difficult. Indeed, an American survey suggested that on average a person with bipolar disorder could expect to lose nine years of life, fourteen years of effective activity and twelve years of normal health. These figures are quoted to emphasise the seriousness of the problem that people with this diagnosis have to deal with. It also shows that there are likely to be important gains to be made for clients who are offered appropriate support and treatment in between episodes as well as when they are clinically depressed or manic.

Possible outcomes

Outcomes can vary widely for people with bipolar disorder. For some people, there will be a small number of episodes at a particular period in their lives and then little impact subsequently. For others, there will be some periods when the illness dominates and other periods when it recedes.

Creativity and bipolar disorder

One of the problems that some people with bipolar disorder describe is that clinicians seem to focus their concern on their highs or manic periods but apparently put less therapeutic effort into helping them with their lows. Whether or not this is always an accurate perception, it highlights an important point. For many people with bipolar disorder, the periods of being manic can be relatively infrequent, or at least short lived, whereas the periods of depression can be more sustained and are often reported as being more painful to the individual.

In between these two extremes is the experience of elevated mood, which is associated with increased levels of mental and physical activity, greater confidence and sociability but which has not developed into mania. People with bipolar disorder often regard this intermediate state of hypomania very positively. During these phases, people will often recall having periods of great creativity either at work or at home and of finding life in general thoroughly enjoyable. Although there is often an awareness that these periods will commonly tip over into a clinical state, it is not uncommon for an individual to aspire to a position in which he or she is able to 'handle' these periods in such a way as to be sustained without becoming ill. Unfortunately, the life histories of many people who have striven to maintain these hypomanic periods at a manageable level show that this is very difficult to achieve.

There is good evidence that many creative people throughout history have had experience of bipolar disorder, including eminent academics, artists, writers, poets and actors. Indeed, the author and psychologist Kay Redfield Jamison, who has written openly about her own experience of bipolar disorder, wrote that she could recall having produced substantial portions of her early work in hypomanic periods. Although she acknowledged the positive side of this, she also identified that the costs increased in terms of further psychiatric episodes and that she has subsequently employed a combination of psychology and drug treatments to maintain mood stability to avoid these costs.

POINTS COVERED IN THIS CHAPTER

1. Bipolar disorder is found in around one in a hundred people at any one time.
2. Symptoms of bipolar disorder include symptoms of both depression (low mood) and mania (elevated mood).
3. Genes can have a role in bipolar disorder, but even people with exactly the same genes do not necessarily all develop the illness.
4. No single specific brain abnormality has been clearly identified in bipolar disorder.
5. Environment and life events (in effect, the experiences that a person has) seem to be important in the development of bipolar disorder.
6. Social and personal costs of bipolar disorder can be severe, but appropriate treatment can improve these outcomes.

7. Periods of increased creativity can occur for some people in hypomania. The costs of trying to maintain this state can be high as, for many people, mania soon develops, often followed by painful periods of depression.

Chapter 2

Treatments for bipolar disorder – medication

For the last fifty years, the first line of treatment for bipolar disorder has consisted, primarily, of the prescription and administration of drugs. The first effective medication for bipolar sufferers, lithium, was introduced in the 1950s and clearly represented a step forward as before this patients could be hospitalised but, once in hospital, there was no effective treatment for them. Certainly medical science has advanced a great deal since that time and a variety of new drugs have been developed. These drugs offer many benefits but also, unfortunately, a number of drawbacks. This chapter offers a brief description of various classes of medication and some of the benefits and drawbacks of each of them, but first we offer a discussion of general issues concerning psychiatric medications for bipolar disorder.

Drug treatments in general

The first point that must be made is that no drug can claim to cure bipolar disorder. As the last chapter explained, the cause of this disorder remains unknown and it seems likely that as long as we do not know the cause or causes, a cure will be impossible to develop. Thus, the drugs described below are *treatments* rather than *cures*. They can be used to relieve symptoms when the person is ill or prevent relapse when he or she is well, but bipolar disorder is a chronic condition that always carries the risk of relapse, and medical science has not been able to alter this fact. In this, bipolar disorder resembles a large number of other illnesses, both mental and physical: schizophrenia, diabetes, asthma, high blood pressure, and Parkinson's disease, to name just a few of the many chronic diseases. These illnesses can all be treated, and often managed successfully for long periods of time, but cannot be cured.

The effectiveness of all drugs varies depending on the person who is taking them, and this is especially true of medications used in psychiatry. Most drugs have a range of dosage at which they can be expected to be effective, and doctors use these guidelines in prescribing. In most cases, drugs taken at these dosages will offer clinical benefit to the patient, although there may also be side effects, as discussed below. However, there are certainly cases in which the benefits are not as great as expected and, as a result, dosages often have to be adjusted for maximum effectiveness. If the side effects are too distressing, the doctor may also suggest a switch to another drug. Thus, drug and dosage have to be determined empirically, meaning that there is often an element of trial and error in arriving at the most effective and tolerable treatment. This can be unnerving for the patient: some patients will say, 'I feel like a guinea pig.' This feeling can be best addressed by collaboration between doctor and patient to arrive at the most effective treatment.

A collaborative approach is also best in dealing with side effects. The term 'side effects' refers to effects of a drug that are unwanted, unpleasant or possibly even harmful. Most medications cause some side effects, for example aspirin can upset the stomach and some hay fever medicines can cause drowsiness. As with the therapeutic effects of drugs, these side effects vary widely from person to person, so that one person may not be troubled at all while taking a particular medication that another patient finds intolerable. With bipolar disorder, a variety of drugs can be prescribed and the patient can work with the doctor to find the most tolerable ones. It is also often the case that side effects occur very quickly, while therapeutic effects may take time, depending on the build-up of drug levels in the body. In addition, sometimes side effects are at their worst at the start of treatment and decrease over the course of one or two weeks. Patients often need to be very patient and put up with weeks of disagreeable side effects in order to see if a particular medication is going to be helpful.

This combination of variable effectiveness and side effects contributes to the problem referred to in the medical literature as the problem of *compliance* or *adherence*: put simply, many patients do not like taking such medications, take them irregularly or refuse to take them altogether. Again, the same effect can be seen in many drugs given for chronic illnesses, especially when the drug does not provide immediate relief from a painful symptom: patients with diseases such as diabetes, asthma or HIV do not like to be reminded that they are ill or different from others, find the drugs unpleasant and may simply forget to take them. For that matter, most of us, when we visit the dentist, are reminded that we have not flossed and brushed our teeth as industriously as we should have. The medical literature demonstrates, again and again, that patients find preventative treatments, treatments that do not immediately relieve symptoms, disagreeable and easy to forget. In addition, taking psychiatric drugs can often be seen as a stigmatised activity, as will be discussed in chapter 10. Further, in some cases of bipolar disorder, the drugs are introduced to the patient during a period of involuntary treatment, and no one likes something that has been forced on them. It is our belief that the bipolar sufferer should carefully consider the pros and cons of taking any medication. Further, if he or she has decided to take any medication, even on a trial basis, that medication should be taken in line with medical recommendations and at the dose prescribed. However, we sympathise with the difficulties that this often involves and the many conflicting feelings that it may produce, such as in the example below.

case

Donald always had mixed feelings about taking lithium. He especially disliked the way it made his hands tremble, as this made him feel very self-conscious, and it also made him feel flat and lacking in creativity. As time went by and he remained well, he worried less and less about falling ill again, and he also found the side effects of lithium more and more annoying. He finally stopped taking it and initially felt much better. He became more sociable and enjoyed his classes more. Unfortunately, this good period was followed by a relapse of his illness. Following this, he went back onto lithium but continued to find it hard to take. Ultimately, he switched to sodium valproate, a drug he has felt much more comfortable taking in the long term.

One final note: most medications have more than one name. Each drug has a scientific name, which is universal, and is also given a trade name by the manufacturer. In some cases, when the drug is not under copyright, several manufacturers may give it different names, though the effectiveness should not differ among different trade names since their manufacture is regulated and uniform. In the following discussion we give both scientific and trade names. However, we do not list all the possible medications in each class of drug, largely because these often change and new drugs are introduced every year. If you would like further information about any drug, your doctor or pharmacist ought to be able to provide it.

Mood stabilisers

These drugs have three uses: during a manic or hypomanic episode they are used to dampen an abnormally high mood; during relatively symptom-free periods they are used to prevent relapses (recurrences) of mania, hypomania and depression; and they can also be used to treat depression in bipolar disorder. They are often not particularly agreeable to take, and patients taking them sometimes complain that they make life feel flat and dull. For this reason, patients taking them over the longer term may fail to take them on a regular basis and thus be at risk of a relapse. It is also worth noting that relapses can occur even in patients who are taking their mood stabilisers as prescribed; such relapses may be the result of stress or a disrupted lifestyle. Even in patients who do relapse, mood stabilisers can increase the time between relapses or decrease the severity of a relapse.

The first mood stabiliser, and the one that is still most commonly prescribed, is *lithium*. It is a naturally occurring element, the lightest of the metals, and commonly found in the form of a salt. An Australian doctor named Cade first discovered, by accident, in the late 1940s that lithium might benefit those suffering from bipolar disorder. Cade's results gradually became more widely known over the following decades, but research done since that time shows that lithium can ameliorate a manic episode and can prevent relapse in a high percentage of those who have suffered from such an episode, and that it can often have benefits in cases of depression. Its mode of action is not completely understood, although progress has been made in this area.

Lithium comes in two forms, lithium carbonate and lithium citrate. It is an effective drug but also a dangerous one, since its toxic level in the blood – the level at which it can endanger the health of the patient – is not far above its therapeutic level – the level it needs to be at to be helpful. For this reason, regular blood tests are essential. It is also important to drink plenty of fluids every day, but alcohol, as well as coffee and strong tea, should be taken in moderation as these drinks can increase urination and cause the body to lose water. Diuretic drugs, and stimulants such as caffeine, which increase urination, should be used with care; make sure to discuss this with your doctor if such drugs are prescribed.

Two other points about lithium are worth making. First, there is evidence that sudden discontinuation of lithium increases the risk of a manic or hypomanic relapse. For this reason, anyone taking lithium who decides to stop it for whatever reason is well advised to do so gradually. Second, some studies have suggested a risk of birth defects in the new-born if a mother is taking lithium during her pregnancy. Newer studies have suggested that this risk is relatively low, but women who take lithium should probably discuss the risks with a doctor before choosing to become pregnant.

drugs

LITHIUM

Common names: Priadel, Camcolit, Litarex, Lithane, Eskalith

Common side effects: Increased thirst and urination, dry mouth, trembling hands, mild nausea, acne

More serious side effects: Weight gain, excessive urination, thyroid and kidney damage

Toxic effects: Persistent diarrhoea, intense thirst, persistent nausea and vomiting, confusion, severe tremor, blurred vision. These symptoms could be a sign of excessive lithium in the blood. **If this condition persists, it could result in kidney damage – consult your doctor.**

Two other drugs are commonly used as mood stabilisers, *sodium valproate* and *carbamazepine*. Both of these were first used for the management of epilepsy, but they have also been found to offer benefits to many bipolar patients. Sodium valproate has been found to be effective in patients who predominantly suffer with depression, whilst carbamazepine works less well in such cases. Like lithium, they need to be monitored and blood tests may be necessary, although the monitoring often does not have to be as strict as in the case of lithium. They also present some risk during pregnancy. As noted above, the patient's own experience of these different drugs is very important in deciding which one is likely to be most effective and most regularly taken.

SODIUM VALPROATE

Common names: Epilim, Divalproex, Depakote

Common side effects: Nausea, vomiting, weight gain, tremors, drowsiness, hair loss

CARBAMAZEPINE

Common name: Tegretol

Common side effects: Dry mouth, nausea, diarrhoea, dizziness, headaches, problems with walking, tiredness, rashes

Antidepressants

Depression has been called 'the common cold of mental illness'. Up to 10% of the population in developed countries may suffer from depression at some point in their lives. As a result, antidepressant drugs are now very widely prescribed. There are a number of different types of antidepressants, but the two most commonly prescribed are the tricyclic antidepressants (TCAs) and the serotonin reuptake inhibitors (SSRIs). The first type has been used for over thirty years and the second for about ten years. Both are equally effective, and both take between two weeks and a month actually to relieve depression. Some patients stop taking their antidepressants before they have had a chance to work. If you are prescribed antidepressants, be sure to take them at the correct dose and do not expect them to work right away! The main difference between these two families of drugs is that they have different side effects. One of the first SSRIs, Prozac, earned a lot of media attention, but it is no more effective than any other antidepressant.

In bipolar disorder, these drugs may be used during depressive episodes. However, there is a risk, in some people, that antidepressants can trigger an episode of mania. Therefore, people with bipolar disorder should probably be on a mood stabiliser when taking antidepressants and, as a rule, not take them for more than six months. Patient and doctor should be aware of this and monitor the patient for early warning signs.

drugs

The TCAs: Examples include amitriptyline (Lentizol/ Elavil), dothiepin/dosulepin (Prothiaden) and lofepramine (Gamanil)

Side effects: These drugs have a wide variety of side effects, which are often worse during the first few weeks, before they begin to have any effect on depression. Common side effects include tiredness and excessive sedation, dry mouth, constipation and difficulty in urinating. After the first few weeks, these side effects should decrease

The SSRIs: Examples include Fluoxetine (Prozac), paroxetine (Seroxat, Paxil), citalopram (Cipramil, Cipram) and sertraline (Lustral, Zoloft). There are also some newer, related antidepressants, including venlafaxine (Efexor) and nefazodone (Dutonin)

Side effects: As noted above, these drugs are said to have fewer side effects than the tricyclics, and they are safer in the event of an overdose. However, they can have a number of varied side effects, including upset stomach, headaches, agitation and rashes. These often subside over time

One other class of antidepressants that are sometimes prescribed is the monoamine oxidase (MAO) inhibitors. These were the first antidepressants, but most of them cannot be mixed with certain foods, such as cheeses and yeast products, and for this reason they are seldom prescribed. However, they have been found to be very effective in some cases of bipolar depression. A new type of MAO inhibitor, moclobemide (Manerix), does not require dietary restriction.

Neuroleptics

These drugs are also referred to as the *antipsychotic* drugs or the *major tranquillisers*. Their principal use is in the treatment of psychosis, and they have been shown to reduce or eliminate many of the symptoms of psychosis, such as bizarre ideas (delusions) or the experience of hearing voices that others do not hear (hallucinations). In bipolar disorder, they are used during acute manic episodes to calm the patient, slow racing thoughts, reduce agitation and help the patient to sleep. Some of the newer antipsychotics have been found to have mood-stabilizing properties, and in recent years have begun to be prescribed as alternatives to the mood stabilizers.

Common neuroleptics include: chlorpromazine (Largactil, Thorazine), haloperidol (Haldol) and trifluoperazine (Stelazine). There are some recently developed neuroleptics, such as risperidone (Risperdal), amisulpride (Solian) and olanzapine (Zyprexa), which are said to have fewer side effects and be easier to take

Side effects: The neuroleptics have many side effects, including sedation (sleepiness), dry mouth, weight gain, constipation and sensitivity to sunlight. A common class of side effects, the so-called extrapyramidal or Parkinsonian side effects, include stiffness and restlessness. These symptoms can be treated with so-called *anti-Parkinsonian* drugs (see below)

Anti-Parkinsonian drugs

As noted above, these drugs are sometimes given with neuroleptic drugs to relieve side effects; they are also known as *anticholinergic* drugs. They are usually not prescribed initially, but only as a treatment for so-called extrapyramidal side effects, if they develop. These effects can include stiffness and rigidity of movement, restlessness, a tremor in the hands and a shuffling walk. Neuroleptics can cause these symptoms in some patients; they usually disappear when the dosage is lowered or stopped, but they can also be treated with anticholinergic drugs. (Please note: Neuroleptic drugs do not cause Parkinson's disease; they can cause symptoms similar to those of Parkinson's disease.)

drugs

Anti-Parkinsonian drugs include: procyclidine (Kemadrin), benzatropine (Cogentin) and benzhexol/trihexphenidl (Broflex)

Side effects: These include dry mouth, stomach upset, dizziness and blurred vision. In some cases these drugs may also create a stimulating, mildly pleasurable effect.

Minor tranquillisers

These medications, also known as the *benzodiazepines*, have been used for years to treat anxiety and insomnia; Valium (diazepam) is one of the best known, but there are many other drugs in the same family. They provide very quick relief for agitation and sleeplessness and, if taken correctly, have very few side effects. Their main problem is the risk of dependency: if taken for insomnia, for example, they may help the patient sleep but will do nothing to solve the underlying problem that may be causing the insomnia. If taken for more than a week or two the patient may become overly reliant on them; if he or she stops taking the tranquilliser, sleep problems or anxiety could return. In bipolar disorder, minor tranquillisers can be used during a manic episode to calm the patient or help with sleep, but they should probably not be used on their own as they do not treat the underlying problem of bipolar disorder or prevent relapse.

drugs

Common benzodiazepines include: diazepam (Valium), lorazepam (Ativan) and clonazepam (Rivotril). Zopiclone (Zimovane) is also used as a hypnotic (sleeping pill), although it is from a different chemical family. The main risk with these drugs is of daytime sedation, with a risk of dependency if used over a prolonged period of time.

Self-monitoring and drug compliance

As will be seen in the chapters that follow, *cognitive-behavioural therapy*, the approach that we believe has much to offer people with bipolar disorder, depends a great deal on monitoring, by the patient, of changes in his or her condition. Self-monitoring can also be helpful for patients who are unsure about whether or not to take medication. We cite the example of Donald, already discussed above. He had many problems with taking lithium, and was initially doubtful about the benefits of sodium valproate. When he started to take sodium valproate, he kept a weekly chart, which was designed to measure both the signs of mania and the main troubling side effects of lithium (see figure 1). After three months, he noted that his scores on most of

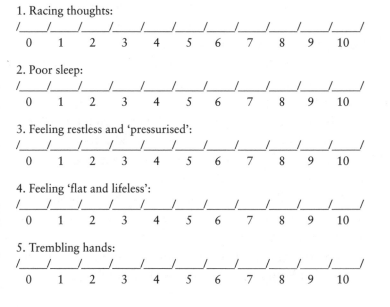

Figure 1 Donald's rating scale for sodium valproate

1. Racing thoughts:

/____/____/____/____/____/____/____/____/____/____/
   0   1   2   3   4   5   6   7   8   9   10

2. Poor sleep:

/____/____/____/____/____/____/____/____/____/____/
   0   1   2   3   4   5   6   7   8   9   10

3. Feeling restless and 'pressurised':

/____/____/____/____/____/____/____/____/____/____/
   0   1   2   3   4   5   6   7   8   9   10

4. Feeling 'flat and lifeless':

/____/____/____/____/____/____/____/____/____/____/
   0   1   2   3   4   5   6   7   8   9   10

5. Trembling hands:

/____/____/____/____/____/____/____/____/____/____/
   0   1   2   3   4   5   6   7   8   9   10

the scales had fallen: for example, he was rating 'poor sleep' at 5 or 6 each week, rather than 8 or 9, and 'trembling hands' at around 3, rather than around 6, as he had on lithium. As a result, he was able to feel more comfortable with the decision to switch to sodium valproate. Thus, self-monitoring – using a scale of one's own devising based on key symptoms and side effects – may offer the person with bipolar disorder a helpful guide when making decisions about medication.

POINTS COVERED IN THIS CHAPTER

1. A number of medications are used in the treatment of bipolar disorder. None of them is a cure, but most people find that some of these medications, alone or in combination, can help them to control their symptoms.
2. All of these medications can cause side effects, but these can often be controlled by careful prescribing.
3. A collaborative relationship between patient and doctor generally produces the best results.
4. Mood stabilisers, such as lithium, are usually the first line of treatment for manic and hypomanic episodes. They can also be used to prevent relapses and treat bipolar depression.
5. Antidepressants are the most common treatment for depression. In bipolar disorder they must be used with care because they can trigger manic episodes.
6. Neuroleptic or antipsychotic drugs are a very effective treatment for mania, especially with psychotic symptoms. Some of the newer ones can also be used as mood stabilizers.
7. Anti-Parkinsonian drugs are used to treat some of the common side effects of neuroleptic drugs.
8. Minor tranquillisers can be used to treat the symptoms of a high, such as agitation and sleeplessness, although they do not affect the manic state itself.
9. Self-monitoring, including the use of questionnaires, can help people to judge if their medications are helpful.

Chapter 3

Treatments for bipolar disorder – professional help

As we have suggested in the previous chapter, a variety of medications exists to help with bipolar disorder, and these can help in a number of ways. However, none of them offers a cure and almost all of them have limitations and drawbacks. As with medication, so with human practitioners: they come in several varieties, they can be very helpful, and they have limitations. Here we offer a brief guide to helping professionals. As a first general comment, we note that most of the mental-health professionals we have known have been hard working and dedicated. We hope that that has been the experience of our readers as well. However, mental-health workers are not saints; they sometimes get things wrong, just as all professionals do. If you have had a bad experience in dealing with a mental-health professional, please do not allow yourself to be prejudiced against all the rest of us. We are sure that if you look assertively for professionals you can work with, you will eventually be able to find a group of workers who can help you.

General practitioners

In the UK, the pathway to any sort of advanced medical help is through one's general practitioner (GP) or family doctor. In general, those seeking specialist help from the mental-health services, or any other sort of specialist help, will have to be referred by a GP. If you believe that you need specialist help, you will need to visit your GP and ask for a referral; that is, a letter to the social services asking that an appointment be sent to you. As with any other illness, you will have to describe your problems and symptoms to the GP. With a case of possible bipolar disorder, most GPs will naturally seek help from specialist psychiatric services. However, there are some GPs with considerable expertise in the field of mental health. Many people prefer to be treated by their GPs, often in consultation with a psychiatrist. Especially if a person is stable on a particular dose of medication – that is, he or she has not fallen ill for some time and has not needed to have an increase or decrease in medication – this can be a very convenient and comfortable arrangement. GPs can certainly prescribe all the necessary medications and order all the necessary tests. The most important considerations are that the patient trusts the doctor and that the doctor has enough expertise and experience to feel comfortable in this role. This is becoming an increasingly popular arrangement, and many community mental health teams (see below) are developing increasingly close links with local GP practices.

Community mental health teams

Increasingly, specialist mental-health treatment is being delivered by *community mental health teams* (CMHTs). As the name suggests, these are teams of professionals based in the community who can offer help to those suffering from serious mental illness. Such teams are often also referred to as *multi-disciplinary teams* because they contain a variety of professionals. Such teams will often be based in a community venue, which might be referred to as a *team base*, where out-patient treatment can be delivered. In the US, public hospitals and HMOs (Health Maintenance Organizations) offer a very similar mix of professionals. In many states there are also community mental health centres where help is available to those who cannot afford medical insurance, although these services are often over-stretched. In this chapter we will outline the training and tasks of the different members of the team as well as saying something about the legal framework of treatment and the rights of people with bipolar disorder. We will also be offering a more extensive discussion of some of these issues later in the book.

Psychiatrists

In our work as clinical psychologists, we are often asked, 'What is the difference between a psychologist and a psychiatrist?' The short answer is that they come to the study and treatment of mental illness through different routes; psychologists through the academic discipline of psychology, which we will say more about below, and psychiatrists through medical training. All *psychiatrists* are qualified medical practitioners, and as such they are licensed to prescribe medications. Although psychiatrists may be trained in other treatment techniques, such as the use of psychological treatments, most psychiatrists see their role as first, the diagnosing of various types of mental illness and, second, the prescribing of appropriate medication. As noted in the previous chapter, prescribing appropriate medication for bipolar disorder is not a simple matter, and a series of appointments may be required while a psychiatrist adjusts the dosage of the medication or medications prescribed. After this, there will generally be follow-up appointments at intervals of a month or longer so that the individual's progress can be monitored and appropriate tests carried out. Psychiatrists generally do not implement psychological treatments, but they can offer useful advice on the management of the illness.

In hospital and clinic settings, there are often a number of psychiatrists with varying grades of seniority. The most senior psychiatrist, the *consultant*, will be in charge of the care of all the people seen by the team; this role is that of the *responsible medical officer* (RMO). Theoretically, he or she will oversee the care of all people being seen by members of the team. However, much of the actual day-to-day work with patients will be carried out by more junior doctors, called *specialist registrars* and *senior house officers*, referred to in the United States as senior residents and residents. These are fully qualified doctors doing advanced training in psychiatry, and they usually rotate between posts, spending six months or a year doing one job and then switching to another one, so that they will be acquainted with all branches of psychiatry. The consultant supervises their clinical work, but they often have considerable medical and psychiatric experience. One disadvantage for people receiving long-term care, especially from a junior doctor, is that they will, over the years, see a variety of doctors instead of being able to get used to one. Many people complain about this but, unfortunately, there are not enough consultants available to allow everybody to be seen regularly by one. An advantage is that this system does produce experienced and knowledgeable consultants. It is worth noting that this system is common to all specialist fields in medicine, not just to psychiatry. Obviously, people who are fortunate enough to have a good private income or health insurance can seek private psychiatric treatment. In the UK, and even more in the US, many fully qualified consultants work either part or full time seeing private patients.

INVOLUNTARY DETENTION

Psychiatrists have a power, that of involuntary detention and treatment, that many patients find intimidating. Ordinary people will sometimes comment to mental-health professionals that they worry that behaving oddly might result in their being 'taken away by men in white coats'. In other words, people believe that psychiatrists have the power to lock people up for any sort of unusual behaviour. This is certainly not the case. Under current mental-health law there are strict limits on involuntary detention. (The correct legal term in Britain is 'detention under a section of the Mental Health Act'; sometimes this is confusing description.) In the UK, for someone to be involuntarily detained, two doctors and a social worker have to agree on three points: first, that the person is suffering from a mental illness in need of treatment; second, that there is a danger to the life or health of either that person or someone else if the illness is not treated; third, that the person is not accepting treatment voluntarily. In other words, mild eccentricities and odd beliefs, in the absence of evidence of harm or danger, are not grounds for involuntary treatment. Further, the detention can only be for set periods of time, and patients can also appeal to an outside agency, the Mental Health Act Tribunal, if they believe their detention is not justified. All mental-health services have Mental Health Act workers who oversee all involuntary detentions. In other words, the ability of psychiatrists to deprive people of their liberty is strictly controlled. American laws are very similar, although the precise details vary from state to state.

Later in this book we offer a fuller discussion of the rights of detained patients. Here we would only like to add that sometimes involuntary detention can be necessary, but that it can also be a very frightening and distressing experience. Anyone who has to spend time in a mental-health facility needs help, sympathy and support, and this is doubly true in the case of someone who is detained against his or her will.

Clinical psychologists

We may have a bit of a prejudice in favour of the next profession discussed, as we are *clinical psychologists* ourselves. It is a relatively new profession, having grown up over the last fifty years out of the academic field of psychology, the study of the mind and behaviour. Clinical psychologists generally practise some form of psychotherapy, which entails trying to help people feel and function better by modifying the ways they think, feel and behave. There are two major forms of psychotherapy, and one of them, psychodynamic psychotherapy, is often referred to simply as psychotherapy, just to confuse matters. We will talk about psychodynamic psychotherapy in a moment. The majority of clinical psychologists use another model of human functioning, called the *cognitive-behavioural model*, which we favour and which is discussed in detail in the next chapter. It is this approach that we believe has a good deal to offer to people with bipolar disorder. Cognitive-behavioural approaches were first used to treat other psychological problems, such as phobias, anxiety and depression, but they have proved useful in treating a wide variety of problems.

Clinical psychologists often practise as part of CMHTs or HMOs, or in clinical psychology departments attached to hospitals and universities. In the UK, people wanting to see a clinical psychologist will usually need a referral letter; that is, a letter from their GP or psychiatrist suggesting that they need treatment. The National Health Service employs a large number of psychologists, but their services are much in demand so there can be a long wait for services. In the US, many psychologists practice in HMOs and all or part of their fees will be covered by health insurance. Of course, people with private means or health insurance can seek private treatment. In that case, it is worth checking to see that the psychologist in question is a chartered clinical psychologist; that is, that their qualification to practise has been endorsed by the British Psychological Society or, in the US, licensed by their state.

Psychodynamic psychotherapists

The oldest form of psychotherapy is psychodynamic psychotherapy, which goes back to Freud. This has various schools of thought, but it has traditionally viewed psychological and psychiatric problems as originating in a person's childhood and development. Courses of therapy are usually longer than with cognitive-behavioural therapy, and the therapy may focus less on specific problems and more on personal relationships. In our clinical work we have met people who have engaged in psychodynamic therapy, and some of them have found it to be very helpful. However, it is our feeling that psychodynamic therapy does not offer a form of therapy aimed specifically at the problems of people with bipolar disorder.

Psychodynamic therapists can be doctors, psychologists or members of other professions. They are sometimes attached to CMHTs or HMOs but are more usually found in hospital or university departments of psychotherapy. Again, one can also seek psychodynamic therapy privately.

Care co-ordinators

Over the last thirty years, with the increasing effectiveness of a variety of psychiatric medications, it has become increasingly unusual for people with serious mental illness to spend very long periods of time in hospital. Hospital admissions are increasingly reserved for periods when the illness is at its worst, and more effort has gone into helping these people to live in the community. The phrase 'care in the community' is often used for this change of emphasis. This approach may not work in every case, but it does work much better than the adverse publicity you can sometimes see in the newspapers might lead you to think.

In the UK, one key part of this approach, called the care programme approach, calls for certain people, usually those who have had one or more hospital admissions, to be monitored while in the community by a care co-ordinator, who is usually a *nurse* or a *social worker*. The care co-ordinator is supposed to meet with the patient regularly, offer advice and support, and make sure that he or she is staying well and receiving appropriate services, and offer guidance on taking medication. If a person is receiving various benefits or having financial problems, a care co-ordinator can offer a great deal of practical support. The care co-ordinator is also supposed to convene regular meetings of all professionals involved in the patient's care, to keep them informed about any changes in the person's situation and to share information. Relatively few people with bipolar disorder are so ill that they need this kind of support. However, for those whose illness is serious and hard to control, and especially for those who do not have a supportive partner or family, the help of a good care co-ordinator can be invaluable. In the US, it is our impression that some state health systems offer similar types of healthcare, but that this system is not as universal as in Britain.

Other members of the multi-disciplinary team

Many of the care co-ordinators in the new CMHTs are *social workers*, but other teams may also have social workers attached to them. Social workers can offer advice, support and counselling, and can help the patient to access various services. In American hospitals, the Social Work Department is often a good place to find out about various types of help available in the community. *Occupational therapists* can also work as care co-ordinators, as well as offering training in a variety of skills ranging from stress management to daily-living skills. With the increasing complexity of the social welfare system, many teams employ a *welfare worker*, who can advise clients about what they are entitled to and how to obtain it. *Resource workers* can advise about courses, charities and other community activities. Finally, most hospitals employ one or more *chaplains*, who have experience talking to people with a mental illness about how their illness may relate to their religious beliefs.

Relationships with professionals

If you are a user of mental-health services, then the chances are that you would rather not be. This is often doubly true of patients who have been involuntarily detained. In such a case, it is natural to be angry at the professionals you are dealing with, and many people are. This may take the form of remembering a specific incident in which a professional seemed rude or uncaring or took an action that you feel was wrong or unhelpful. If this happens, you of course have the right to complain. All hospitals, CMHTs and HMOs have complaints procedures, and patients can always request a change in their doctor or care co-ordinator without jeopardising their care. However, we urge you to think carefully about asking for such a change. If your problem results from a particular episode or action by a staff member, a good first step might be to talk to that person, explain your feelings and ask for an apology. If you find one particular person hard to deal with, then by all means ask for another worker instead. But if your problem is a general one, it may still be there when you are working with a new person. In that case, a whole new way of dealing with your illness may be called for. This book will offer you some ideas about how to do this.

Occasionally the opposite problem may arise: some patients may develop strong positive feelings for a professional. Perhaps your consultant comes to seem like a wise, caring father so that you cannot bear the thought of his retiring; perhaps your care co-ordinator is so sensitive and attractive that you begin to have romantic thoughts about her. This is natural, but you should bear in mind that all the caring professions have strong ethical and professional prohibitions against the development of personal relationships – especially romantic or sexual ones – with clients. If you find that such feelings are interfering with your care, you should probably discuss them with the person involved. Should any professional seem to suggest that he or she might be interested in a more personal relationship, beware; that person is breaking professional rules and could be banned from practising as a result.

POINTS COVERED IN THIS CHAPTER

1. Virtually all people with bipolar disorder will have contact with their doctor. Many people prefer treatment by their doctor if this is possible and many CMHTs and HMOs are working with doctors to support this.

2. CMHTs and HMOs contain a range of professionals, often including psychiatrists, clinical psychologists, social workers and psychiatric nurses.
3. The primary roles of the psychiatrist are those of diagnosis and treatment with medication.
4. Psychiatrists have the power to detain people only in clearly defined and restricted situations determined by law.
5. Clinical psychologists tend to specialise in the application of psychological therapies to people's problems. The most promising psychological treatment for bipolar disorder is, we believe, cognitive-behavioural therapy.
6. Care co-ordinators are named individuals within CMHTs, usually nurses or social workers, who help to co-ordinate the input from other professionals within and outside the team in helping individual patients.
7. Relationships with the professionals responsible for your care are important. Sometimes there can be problems in these relationships that can be resolved by discussion or work with different personnel. Where problems occur in which there is a risk of personal rather than professional relationships forming, it is the responsibility of the professional to avoid this happening as it is contrary to the professional codes of practice.

Chapter 4

Recent developments in psychological approaches to bipolar disorder

Recent developments

Recently there has been increasing interest in developing psychological interventions specifically for bipolar disorder. This is because of the recognition that mood stabilisers (i.e. medication to prevent relapses) fail between 20% to 40% of classical bipolar patients. There is much room for improving the treatment of bipolar disorder.

Almost all the recent developments combine psychotherapy with medication in order to prevent relapses. These approaches are based on the assumption that medication will help the biological aspects of the illness whereas psychotherapy may help the individual to lead a life that avoids unnecessary stress or to deal with unavoidable stress better in order to avoid relapses. This type of approach is well summarised by a patient's thoughts from a classic textbook written by Goodwin and Jamison (1990):

> Medication may prevent my seductive but disastrous high, diminishes my depressions, clears out the wool and webbing from my disordered thinking, slows me down, gentles me out, keeps me from ruining my career and relationship, keeps me out of hospitals, alive and makes psychotherapy possible. But ineffably, psychotherapy heals. It makes some sense of the confu-

sion, reins in the terrifying thoughts and feelings, returns some control and opens the possibility of learning from it all. [...] No pills can help me deal with the problem of not wanting to take pills; likewise, no amount of analysis alone can prevent my manias and depressions. I need both.

As stated in chapter 1, genes play a significant role in the illness. However, stresses in the person's life, particularly stresses that may upset the vulnerable individual's sleep-and-wake cycle, can often trigger the onset or recurrence of the illness. Since some stress is unavoidable in life, psychotherapy in bipolar disorder also aims to help the individual to cope with stress in a more adaptive way. Moreover, these relapse-prevention approaches advocate dealing with the symptoms at an early stage of an episode so that the patient can use psychological techniques to tackle these early warning signs and to 'nip it in the bud'. We also advocate that patients should engage in psychotherapy when they are not in an acute stage, i.e. not *deeply* depressed or in a full-blown manic state. This reasoning is based on the clinical observation that when patients are in a full-blown manic episode, it is often harder to engage them. Furthermore, when patients are in acute episodes, it may not be the optimal time for them to learn relapse-prevention techniques. However, this does not mean that patients should be totally symptom-free when they engage in psychotherapy. More often than not, bipolar patients have residual symptoms or short-lived mood swings even when they are not in an acute episode. In fact, it is important that there are some symptoms so that therapists and patients can work together to deal with them. As long as patients are not manic or deeply depressed, most therapists are happy to engage patients for relapse-prevention therapy. As mentioned above, part of relapse-prevention is to tackle early warnings of an episode promptly. This idea of early treatment has a similarity with the treatment of physical illness; it is often more effective to treat an illness at an early stage before the patient develops a full-blown illness.

Two types of psychotherapy are being developed for bipolar patients: *interpersonal psychotherapy* and *cognitive-behavioural therapy*. Both therapies have been proved to be effective in treating unipolar depression (i.e. depression without mania or hypomania). Interpersonal psychotherapy is being developed in Pittsburgh in the US by a team led by Dr Ellen Frank. The study is well organised and at the time of writing this chapter, no preliminary results have yet been published. In contrast, there are three studies on cognitive-behavioural therapy for bipolar disorder (Lam *et al.*, 2000, 2003 and Scott *et al.*, 2001). Both types of therapy require trained therapists. We shall concentrate on cognitive-behavioural therapy since this is more commonly available in Britain and elsewhere. However, we should watch out for the results of the interpersonal psychotherapy study.

What is cognitive-behavioural therapy?

Cognitive-behavioural therapy is a form of psychotherapy that aims to empower people by teaching them how to deal with maladaptive emotions and preventing future relapses. Typically, a course of cognitive-behavioural therapy is between twelve and eighteen sessions. Therapy focuses on the 'here and now'. The past is examined in order to understand and put into context the present problems.

Cognitive-behavioural therapy is problem-orientated. Patients and therapists work as a team to deal with some of the problems patients have. Therapists and patients often agree on certain tasks that patients carry out in between sessions so that patients can practise what they learn in therapy, and sometimes these tasks can serve the function of gathering information for therapy sessions.

Thoughts, mood and behaviour

Cognitive-behavioural therapy is based on the simple principle that our thinking, behaviour and emotions can affect each other.

Most of us have experienced occasions when we did not want to go out because we felt slightly low and could not be bothered, yet when we actually went out, we enjoyed ourselves and felt better (an example of behaviour affecting mood). On the other hand, most of us also have experienced the 'low' occasions when we decided against going out and sat at home 'like a lemon'. We did not feel any better and in fact felt more miserable. Thinking can also affect mood. Here is an example: you are watching television alone at home on a dark evening. There is nobody else in the house. Suddenly, you hear a loud noise in the kitchen. You think it is a burglar. You will probably be scared and want to run to safety. However, if, instead of thinking it was a burglar, you had thought it was your cat knocking a vase onto the floor, you may feel irritated. You may rush into the kitchen to see what has happened, with the intention of putting the cat out of the house. The situation in these two scenarios is the same. The only difference is your thought, i.e. your interpretation of the situation.

In clinically depressed patients, these principles also hold. It is well established that when people are depressed, they have more negative or depressing thoughts. When people are euphoric, their thoughts can be more optimistic. In extreme emotional states, these thoughts can be unrealistically depressing or optimistic and can pop into the mind without any real effort. Cognitive-behavioural therapists call these 'automatic thoughts'. Furthermore, in extreme emotional states, these thoughts can become very real to the patient, despite objective evidence to the contrary. This in turn can make the emotional state even more extreme. For example, when depressed, the patient may have self-accusatory thoughts that his or her depression is a result of being weak or useless and, as a result of these negative thoughts, become more depressed. When high, the patient may believe that he or she has unusual abilities and get very irritated when others do not understand, or take a different view. The patient becomes more elated because of this belief of possessing unusual abilities, and irritated with people perceived as less able, who yet refuse to follow the patient's ideas.

How does cognitive-behavioural therapy work?

Cognitive-behavioural therapists do not assume that the mood disorder is caused solely by problematic thoughts or behaviours, but most cognitive-behavioural therapists agree that certain behaviour or thinking can at least maintain the disorder. Hence, therapists and patients work together to tackle these behaviours or thinking. In bipolar disorder, therapists and patients also examine behaviour that may trigger further episodes or make the patient vulnerable to relapses.

In cognitive-behavioural therapy, patients are first taught to monitor thoughts and behaviour. They are taught to catch these automatic thoughts as they occur and write them down. They are also taught to monitor their behaviour or activities by filling in a record. Then later, thoughts and behaviours are used to influence mood. Patients are taught how to deal with these automatic thoughts through techniques that enable them to step aside and examine the reality of these thoughts.

The following case vignette shows how Melissa and her therapist worked together to help Melissa step aside and examine the reality of her negative automatic thoughts. Melissa describes how she was very depressed one day because she had lost an account at work.

case

Melissa: *I was very depressed at work last Tuesday. I lost an important account for my firm. I have worked very hard at getting the business.*

Therapist: *I can see in your thought record that you rated your depression 90 out of 100 on that day.*

Melissa: *Yes, I could not get it out of my mind.*

Therapist: *Let us look at your thought records. Your automatic thought was 'I am a failure and a burden to the company. John (a colleague) will be better off without me. The firm would also do better.' And the strength of your beliefs was about 85% for each thought.*

Melissa: *Yes.*

Therapist: *Let us examine these thoughts and look at the objective evidence. First of all, if John lost an account and said he was a failure and a burden to you, what would you say?*

Melissa: *I would say that he is not. He is good at running projects and very methodical in his work. I would not call him a burden. Losing accounts is part of life in our business.*

Therapist: *Does it not apply to you? When was the last time you pulled something off?*

Melissa: *Only last month. I did get a couple of new accounts. However, this one I lost was an important one.*

Therapist: *Sure. Losing something big is always disappointing. However, did John say anything about it?*

Melissa: *Yes, he was also disappointed. However, he also said that you win some and you lose some.*

Therapist: *Is it not true? How is business doing recently?*

Melissa: *Not too bad. We are doing better than last year.*

Therapist: *Who pulled in most of the accounts?*

Melissa: *In my department I suppose I did. I am more outgoing and more experienced in dealing with people. John is better at getting things done.*

Therapist: *So what does it say about you two working as a team?*

Melissa: *I suppose it does mean that we are a good team.*

Therapist: *So what conclusion can we draw from our discussion?*

Melissa: *I suppose the conclusion is that losing business is part of life. It does not mean that I am a failure and a burden. John and I make a good team.*

Therapist: *How much do you believe in what you just said?*

Melissa: *About 70%.*

Therapist: *How would you rate your mood now as a result of our discussion?*

Melissa: *about 40% depressed.*

Therapist: *I wonder in the past when you lost a big project, did you always conclude that you were a burden and a failure?*

Melissa: *Only if I am a bit low as I have been recently.*

Therapist: *Sure. That is a very good example of how if we are feeling a bit low, we tend to blame ourselves and jump to a negative conclusion.*

Patients are also taught to regulate their activity levels and to learn to use behaviour to influence their mood. When patients are depressed, they tend to disengage from pleasurable activities or activities that might give them a sense of achievement. Tasks are frequently left undone because depressed patients lack energy and see tasks as insurmountable. Therapists often use behavioural techniques such as engaging in enjoyable activities or graded tasks (small goal-directed steps) to help these patients pull themselves out of their depression somewhat. In a mildly high state (hypomanic state), therapists often persuade patients to act against their instinct of going out and seeking more stimulation. Instead, they are persuaded to do less and engage in calming activities to prevent further stimulation that might lead to an even more euphoric state.

The next case vignette follows on from a session Donald has had with his therapist after he was in a slightly 'high' mood the previous week. He was more chatty than usual in the therapy session. On questioning, he admitted to being more aroused. Colours were more vivid to him and he could see advertisements on the roadside as particularly funny. In the past, these had been the early warnings that he might be going into a manic episode. It was therefore suggested in the session that Donald focus on calming activities and on avoiding situations in which there was a risk of becoming over-stimulated. Here is their next meeting:

Therapist: *How have you been since we last met?*

Donald: *Better. I am much calmer now.*

Therapist: *I am pleased to hear that. What happened?*

Donald: *I went home as we discussed here and stayed at home instead of going out. I also cancelled my choir practice as I can get very stimulated by religious ideas when I am slightly high. I also took a sleeping pill and made sure that I had a good night sleep. I have been careful not to seek out simulating activities all week. As a result I feel much calmer.*

Assumptions

Our mood and behaviour are governed by rules and values we have as people. These rules and values are called assumptions. However, if these assumptions become too rigid or absolute and stop us achieving our goals, we call them dysfunctional assumptions. They are called dysfunctional because they become a burden and hinder us in achieving what we want to achieve. Examples of these rules are: 'If I try hard enough, I should be able to excel at anything I attempt'; 'I cannot be happy unless I am loved'; 'I am nothing unless I achieve'; 'Things are not worth doing unless I do them perfectly'. They can also be very rigid: 'I should be happy all the time'; 'I should have control of what happens to me.' As a result of such rules, a person may get into all types of dysfunctional behaviours. For example, a person who believes that 'I should be able to *excel at anything* I attempt if I try hard enough' may get into very driven behaviour and be very upset at any setbacks, which are defined as anything in which he or she does not excel. Hence, being 'good' is not enough and is classified as a setback. The way the person deals with setbacks may be to try even harder.

The following case vignette illustrates how Melissa has coped with any setback in the past. She has this belief that 'If I try hard enough, I should be able to excel at anything I attempt.'

case

Melissa: *If I have any setbacks at work, the way I cope is to take on something more difficult so that I could 'make good' my setback. I will take on something bigger and sometimes two or more of those tasks.*

Therapist: *What happened in the past when you did that?*

case

Melissa: *I would get into an aroused state and feeling very stretched. In the past, when it was really bad, I would drink. Alcohol was a fuel to keep me going.*

Therapist: *What happened next?*

Melissa: *I would fail more and take on more until I could not cope. Then I crash down into a depression.*

As therapy progresses, therapists and patients then work together to focus more on these 'dysfunctional assumptions' in order to change the long-standing pattern of thought and behaviour. Therapists may help patients to examine the pros and cons of such beliefs and engage in new and more adaptive behaviour. For example, a person with high and unrealistic standards may be persuaded to examine the pros and cons of this. One disadvantage may be procrastination, leading to the result that the person does not get a lot of tasks completed. The therapist might be able to persuade the person to complete tasks to a 'good enough' standard in order to experience getting assignments completed on time.

POINTS COVERED IN THIS CHAPTER

1. Psychotherapy for bipolar disorder is usually a combination of psychotherapy and medication.
2. These approaches are based on the assumption that medication will help the biological aspect of the illness whereas psychotherapy may help the individual to lead a life that avoids unnecessary stress or to handle stress better.
3. Two types of psychotherapies are being developed for bipolar patients: interpersonal psychotherapy and cognitive-behavioural therapy. Both therapies have been proved to be effective in treating unipolar depression (i.e. depression without mania or hypomania).

4. Cognitive-behavioural therapy is more commonly available than interpersonal psychotherapy in Britain and some parts of the United States.

5. Cognitive-behavioural therapy aims to empower patients by giving them the tools to deal with maladaptive emotions and to prevent future relapses. Therapy is problem-orientated and focuses on the 'here and now'.

6. Patients are also taught to regulate their activity levels and to learn to use behaviour and thinking to influence their mood.

7. Cognitive-behavioural therapists do not assume that the mood disorder is caused solely by problematic thoughts or behaviour. However, most cognitive-behavioural therapists agree that certain behaviour or thinking can at least maintain the disorder.

8. Cognitive-behavioural therapy is based on a simple principle that our thinking, behaviour and emotions can affect each other.

9. Our mood and behaviour are governed by rules and values we have as people. These rules and values are called assumptions. However, if these assumptions become too rigid or absolute, and stop us achieving our goals, we call them dysfunctional assumptions.

10. As therapy progresses, therapists and patients work together to focus more on the 'dysfunctional assumptions' in order to change the long-standing pattern of thought and behaviour.

Chapter 5

Early warnings

Monitoring moods and early warning signs

Medication compliance is an important factor in determining how bipolar patients fare. However, the patients who do really well are those who have learnt to monitor their moods and to watch out for early warning signs. Monitoring mood can be quite complicated. Some patients are very scared about any mood fluctuations, some of which may be the daily ups and downs everyone feels. In general, as long as the mood is not too extreme and as long as you can link it to something that has happened in your life, you should not be too worried about it. However, if the mood swings are extreme and often out of proportion to any reasonable causes, then we generally advise patients to be more careful. Some patients, however, have learnt to observe their moods in very sophisticated ways. The following case vignette describes a patient's experience and demonstrates how she monitors her mood and looks out for trends over days.

case

Melissa: *Yes. I do monitor my mood. Over the last couple of years, I learnt that realising that I have a serious illness and need medication is a first step. It helps to cut out the rough edges of the ups and downs in my mood. However, monitoring my mood is important. It gives me a sense of control and helps me to detect any early warning signs and prevent them from developing into a full-blown illness. Undetected illness can ruin my career and wreck my relationships.*

Therapist: *How do you do it?*

Melissa: *I monitor my mood every day. For example, it is all right to be happy after a skiing holiday. But if my mood keeps going up for several days for no obvious reasons, then I know I have to be careful.*

Early warning signs tend to be very different from patient to patient. In fact, this is the case for most forms of mental illness. Some people call these idiosyncratic warning signs 'individual relapse signatures'. In monitoring early warning signs for bipolar illness, we tend not to use mood as a pointer. Mood is a bit more difficult to gauge. Instead, we tend to be as specific as possible in describing the social context in which these early warning signs manifest themselves. Hence, instead of encouraging a statement such as 'I am more irritable', we would ask how the irritability would show itself, or with whom the patient would be irritable. Of course, any one sign may not mean a lot. We tend to map out a combination of early warning signs – the individual relapse signature.

Early warning signs of mania

As mentioned above, early warning signs are different from patient to patient. The most common early warnings of mania are:

- not being interested in sleep, or sleeping less
- engaging in more projects or activities
- being more sociable

- thoughts start to race
- being more irritable
- being more optimistic
- being more excitable and restless.

There is evidence that bipolar patients tend to report similar patterns of early warnings consistently over time even though individual patterns are unique to a person. It is important to note that most of these early warnings for mania are behavioural in nature. Hence, patients' close relatives or friends can help in detecting these early signs. However, this has to be done in a sensitive way. In our experience, it is best for patients to have a frank discussion with people who are close to them if they want to enlist their help. It is also important to have agreement about how the person helping will express his or her concern without the patient feeling resentful about it. There is no one way of doing this. Each person is different.

The following case vignette illustrates how Melissa discusses with her husband how he can help her to detect early warnings.

case

Melissa: *I had a discussion with my therapist and we thought maybe it would be a good idea if you and I can work together to help me to detect any early warning signs of relapse.*

Husband: *It sounds good to me. However, you have not always wanted to hear it. In the past you were irritated with me for expressing concern.*

Melissa: *Yes. It is hard to hear these things, particularly if I am feeling good. However, I was really feeling scared and lonely whenever I was unwell. I know you have always been there for me. But it is also hard for me to reach out.*

Husband: *You know that you are not alone. Tell me what I can do.*

Melissa: *If we start off by you helping me to detect the early warning signs, I will feel that we are tackling the illness together.*

Husband: *I am more than willing to do that. What can I say that may make you feel I am not interfering?*

Melissa: *I will probably feel less resentful since we have talked about it now. However, in the past, what really irritated me was when you say 'Are you alright? Should you be seeing a doctor?' It will help if you can be more specific about it.*

Husband: *What can I say instead?*

Melissa: *Perhaps you can say something like: 'I noticed that you have not been sleeping well and you have been going through a difficult period at work. Do we need to slow down?' It does not always mean I am ill. Sometimes it comes to nothing.*

Husband: *It's fine. I was only concerned. I do sometimes jump to conclusions. However, I need to be able to ask if you need to see a doctor when I am really concerned.*

Melissa: *Yes, I understand that. My therapist and I are working out a list of early warnings and part of coping better with the illness is to see a doctor early. Perhaps you can have a contribution there. I will show you the sheet of paper and see what you think when we finish the first draft.*

Since these early warnings are vague by nature, we find that it is important to anchor them in some personal context. Some patients can also pinpoint the stressful antecedents or situations, such as a demanding period at work, that can lead to the identification of early warnings.

The following case vignette demonstrates how Melissa and her therapist work together to be more specific about her early warning signs of irritability.

case

Therapist: *One of your early warning signs of getting high is being irritable. It is a mood and some patients find it difficult to gauge it. I wonder if we can be more specific about this.*

Melissa: *Yes. Doesn't everyone become irritable from time to time without necessarily going high?*

Therapist: *Good point. I guess the answer is that being irritable on its own may not necessarily be an early warning. However, if you feel the need for less sleep, start taking on more tasks and being irritable, then perhaps you need to be a bit careful.*

Melissa: *I see what you mean. We are talking about the pattern of early warning signs that are unique to myself.*

Therapist: *Yes. Perhaps we can think who are the people you are irritable with at the early stage.*

Melissa: *At the very early stage, I am irritable with my husband. Then, as it gets worse, I am irritable with my daughter and finally, if I am really bad, I am irritable with my colleagues.*

In fact, Melissa's early warning signs of mania consist of the following.

First stage (lasting 5 days):
- sleeping for less than five hours for more than three nights;
- being more irritable with her daughter and husband;
- talking to neighbours she does not normally talk to;
- being over-enthusiastic about gardening (digging continuously for the whole afternoon).

Second stage (lasting 5 to 8 days):
- being irritable with colleagues;
- talking to strangers in the street;
- sleeping for less than four hours for three nights;
- uncharacteristically for her, having more than two ongoing projects;
- being very distractible.

Coping with early warnings of mania

Once patients have identified that they are in an early stage of an episode, they are taught by cognitive-behavioural therapists how to deal with the illness. Again, the principle is how thought and behaviour can affect mood. In the case of mania, the general principles include:

- avoiding further stimulation;
- engaging in calming activities;
- doing the minimal amount that is essential;
- taking extra precautions to ensure adequate rest and sleep.

Some patients deliberately make sure they take a lunch break even though the temptation is to use every minute of the day to work. When being a bit high, the common thought when awake at 4.00 a.m. is 'Great, I feel full of energy. I have several extra hours to complete the job I am doing.' Patients are taught deliberately to rest in bed even if they cannot sleep.

One temptation when going 'high' is to enjoy it. This is particularly the case when patients have been in a long spell of depression. However, most patients know when they are going 'high' rather than recovering from a depression, especially as they do not have a sense of euphoria and an unrealistic optimism in the recovering. It is always best to check it out with your therapist, nurse or psychiatrist when in doubt.

Getting an early appointment to seek medical help is desirable. Some patients have a good relationship with their prescribing physician, involving mutual trust and respect. It is not uncommon in such a case for the physician to prescribe a low dose of sedative so that the patient can take it on detection of early warnings. Likewise, sleeping tablets are sometimes prescribed so that the patient can break the pattern of insomnia. In either case, it is important for the patient to have a good discussion with the physician about when to take the extra tablets. A study done in Manchester, UK (Perry *et al.*, 1999) investigated whether teaching bipolar patients to detect early warning signs and seek medical help was beneficial to patients. It was found that this type of approach helped to prevent mania episodes, not bipolar depression.

Early warning signs of depression

The most common early warning signs of depression are:

- loss of interest in activity
- loss of interest in people
- inability to put worries or anxieties aside
- interrupted sleep
- desire to cry
- low motivation

There is evidence that early warnings of depression are more difficult to detect than those of mania. This is probably because of the nature of depression itself. Compared with mania, depression tends to be more insidious in onset. Some patients' experience is that 'Depression is like a virus. It creeps up on you. And you just wake up with it.' Another difficulty is that some patients have some depression symptoms left from a previous depression (residual depression). A lot of the early warning signs of depression are very similar to these residual depression symptoms. Hence, it is difficult to gauge when these residual depression symptoms become early warnings. However, our experience is that with help from their cognitive-behavioural therapists and close others, most patients can learn to identify early warnings of depression.

The following is Laverne's list of early warnings of depression.

First stage (lasting 14 days):
- feeling tired;
- feeling very relaxed about housework;
- going quiet and not being talkative;
- sleeping more over the weekend (going to bed in the day).

Second stage (lasting 8 to 10 days):
- being anti-social, not wanting to go out to see friends;
- withdrawing from daughter;
- being impatient with everyone;
- not answering the phone.

Coping with early warnings of depression

The general principles of coping with depression are:

- do enough to keep going so that tasks do not mount up;
- break large tasks into smaller ones and tackle the small projects one at a time;
- engage in some activities to make you feel you are still getting a sense of achievement;
- evaluate your achievement in the context of how low you feel;
- get social support and companionship;
- do activities that may give you some pleasure;
- talk to partners or close friends about your worries.

Our advice is that when you are slightly depressed, the one thing you should not do is to be on your own ruminating about how you feel. Depression is an illness. It does not make anybody a failure or a weak person. Furthermore, depression makes your thinking a bit 'off the rail'. It does not mean you are mad. As stated previously, our mood always biases our thinking; this is normal. In depression, biased thinking is more exaggerated. Talking about your worries to other people is often a good idea. The other person can often 'inject' some reality into your worries. Moreover, you should always evaluate what you have achieved in the context of your being depressed.

The following case vignette illustrates how, with her therapist's help, Laverne evaluates what she has done in the context of her depression.

Laverne: *I did what we agreed. I started organising my papers and paid two bills.*

Therapist: *How do you feel about it?*

Laverne: *It feels OK.*

Therapist: *You don't sound very pleased. Do you remember why we agreed on the assignment?*

Laverne: *Yes. It is to make a start in tackling some real concerns about things I have neglected recently.*

Therapist: *It sounds like you have reservations.*

Laverne: *No, but it is nothing to boast about. These are tasks I should be able to do. In fact, I could have done it in half the time.*

Therapist: *True, you might be able to achieve that in half of the time if you are not depressed. However, you are now depressed. One of the effects of depression is to make people slow down and concentration is always a problem when people are depressed. You should evaluate what you have done in that context. Supposing you broke a leg and the leg is in plaster. Would you kick yourself for not running the marathon when you are just beginning to go out on your own without assistance?*

Laverne: *I see what you mean. It goes back to the idea of taking things on gradually.*

This chapter has described some general principles of how you can monitor your mood, detect early warnings of relapses and respond to these early warnings in an adaptive way. These activities involve a lot of skill. The principles sound simple; however, the execution of these skills is rather complex and needs practice. It is desirable to see a cognitive-behavioural therapist to help you with it. Finally, in addition to dealing with these early warnings in an adaptive way, we also advise patients to see a doctor at an early stage so that if medication is needed, it can be prescribed promptly.

POINTS COVERED IN THIS CHAPTER

1. Patients who do really well are those who have learnt to monitor their moods and to watch out for early warning signs.
2. Monitoring mood can be very complicated. Some patients are scared about any mood fluctuations, some of which are the daily ups and downs everyone feels.
3. In general, as long as the mood is not too extreme and as long as you can link it to events that are happening in your life, you should not be too worried.
4. It is advisable to be cautious about extreme mood swings, particularly those that are out of proportion to any reasonable causes.

5.   Early warning signs tend to be very different from patient to patient. Some people call these idiosyncratic warning signs 'individual relapse signatures'.

6.   In monitoring early warning signs for bipolar illness, we try to be as specific as possible in describing the social context in which these early warning signs manifest themselves.

7.   The most common early warnings for mania are: not being interested in sleep, or sleeping less; engaging in more projects or activities; being more sociable; thoughts start to race; being more irritable; being more optimistic; being more excitable and restless.

8.   Once patients have identified that they are in an early stage of an episode, they are taught by cognitive-behavioural therapists how to deal with the illness.

9.   In the case of mania, the general principles include: avoiding further stimulation; engaging in calming activities; doing the minimal amount that is essential; taking extra precautions to ensure adequate rest and sleep.

10. The most common early warning signs for depression are: loss of interest in activities; loss of interest in people; inability to put worries or anxieties aside; interrupted sleep; desire to cry; low motivation.

11. The general principles of coping with depression are: do enough to keep going so that tasks do not mount up; break large tasks into smaller ones and tackle the small projects one at a time; get social support and companionship; talk to partners or close friends about your worries.

12. Monitoring of mood and detecting early warnings of relapses involve a lot of skill. It takes practice and is desirable to see a cognitive-behavioural therapist to help you with it. In the cases of having detected early warnings both of mania and of depression, we also advise patients to see a doctor at an early stage so that if medication is needed, it can be prescribed promptly.

Chapter 6

Helping yourself – routine, diet and relaxation

We said in the introduction to this book that it is important if you have a diagnosis of bipolar disorder that you have an active role in your own treatment. That means you as an individual taking responsibility, when well, for some of the choices you make. There are some practical areas in which a sensible approach can act to help protect you from harmful mood changes. We do not pretend that these are alternatives to more traditional approaches (such as drug treatment), but, rather, that they can give additional benefits.

We are well aware that many people with a diagnosis of bipolar disorder are independent, strong-minded people for much of the time. This is a good thing, generally, but may initially lead to the feeling that some of the suggestions below seem boring or restrictive. This is not our intention; rather, we would aim for people to be able to maximise their choices, but in a way that also allows them to minimise the risks of ill health and the costs this brings. Many patients have said that the intoxication of a high was matched only by the pain of the crash in mood that followed, and, with it, the disruption of family, work and home.

Protective effects of routine

A regular routine is important in staying well. This means that when sleep, eating and exercise happen on a reasonably regular basis for you, this will help to keep your mood within limits that feel acceptable to you. The effect of a chaotic lifestyle is, conversely, to put you at greater risk of more severe mood changes. The importance of the body clock is described in more detail in chapter 8. It seems that one of the important reasons for having a routine is so that you can notice when mood changes that are out of the ordinary are beginning. One of the problems with a more spontaneous (or chaotic) lifestyle is in the randomness of the ups and downs that occur, making it difficult to notice such mood changes until they have already started to be a problem.

Although routine is important, this does not mean that you should do the same things every day, or that you should never act in a spontaneous manner. It is much more about attaining a balance. Having a sleep routine does not mean going to bed at exactly the same time every night, but it does mean that fluctuating between 9.00 p.m. one night and 3.00 a.m. another night is not a good idea. Similarly, with eating it is beneficial that there are three eating periods in the day and that these are at the beginning of the day, somewhere in the middle of the day, and then towards the end of the day. It is the presence of these 'anchor points' that is important rather than the precise time at which they occur. Also, if you manage to keep a routine of this type most of the time, on the odd occasions when things are more chaotic, there will tend to be less impact, as long as such periods are brief. The following example shows how helpful such a routine can be.

case
When Melissa first started working in advertising, the culture at her office was one of long hours, working through lunch and often socialising with clients after work. Although she initially enjoyed this, it began to cause her problems over time as her mood became more erratic and it became harder for her to manage her work and home life. In discussions with her therapist, the hectic and

erratic pattern of her routines was noted and plans were made for changes. It was agreed that Melissa would begin by taking at least two breaks during the working day and that socialising after work (and associated drinking) would be reduced to a couple of times per week. This would allow time for rest and also for resolving practical issues at home that had mounted up as she was always at work. The spur for these changes was Melissa's own observation of the problems her lifestyle was causing. Initially, she was concerned about how her colleagues would respond to these changes, but she was also aware that if she carried on as she was she might be putting her career at risk. In fact, although her colleagues did comment on the fact that she was going out less, they came to accept it. The outcome for Melissa was positive in that the stress of unpaid bills at home was sorted out in the extra time she had available and she found that having predictable rest periods at work and home led to her feeling more refreshed and creative and therefore more confident in her job role.

Eating well and feeling well

When you do things is important, as noted above. What you do matters as well. Food, for instance, is a vital issue. This is not unique to people with a diagnosis of bipolar disorder, of course. It is, however, more likely that if you are battling with mood difficulties, some of the basics might get overlooked.

We have found that many people we have worked with have tended to get distracted from maintaining a healthy diet. This can be because their mood is fluctuating, or because mood is low and it feels too difficult, or because when mood is reasonable, there seem to be too many other things to be getting on with. So, with most people, it is not that they do not know about healthy eating but that they need to remind themselves to do this. It can therefore be useful to set aside some time each week to plan out what you might need to buy so that you have a choice of fruit, vegetables, cereals and meat (or alternatives if you are vegetarian). This can then be part of a routine, rather than something that is thought about at the last minute. Often, this planning time is well spent and can lead both to a more balanced diet and to more time being available for the other 'more important' things that most of us want to be getting on with.

A healthy diet is about eating a range of foods, including fresh fruit and vegetables, and not relying too heavily on foods heavy in saturated fats (such as fried food and many take-away meals). If you eat a balanced diet on a regular basis, it will have an impact on mood. This is because when your physical system is functioning well on the proper 'fuel', it works more efficiently, whereas if it is below par, it can be associated with feelings of being low or under the weather.

Another reason why a healthy diet affects mood is that there is a psychological importance attached to treating yourself in a positive manner. If you regularly take the time and effort to treat yourself well in this way, a message is sent to you that you are worth the effort. The more often this message is sent, the more likely it is that it will be picked up psychologically. People who feel that they are worth the effort tend to feel better about themselves and thus tend generally to be in better spirits than those who habitually behave in an 'it's only me so I won't bother' way, as the following example illustrates.

case | *Laverne found it difficult to generate the energy to buy and cook good food. She was careful to provide well for her daughter, but struggled to do so for herself. She felt that she couldn't afford to eat 'proper food' and therefore got used to living on snacks. As her diet was so poor, it seemed likely that this would be making her ongoing difficulties with low mood worse. Efforts were made in working with Laverne to come up with a practical plan to provide a reasonable diet for herself that was not too arduous to prepare and fell within her limited budget. Plans were drawn up between Laverne, her therapist and her dietician. Initially, it was agreed to do this for a trial period of a month. Laverne agreed that if this change helped her mood over that period, she would continue with it afterwards; if it did not, she would return to her previous 'easy' pattern of eating. Over this period, Laverne rated her mood daily and this provided clear evidence of an improvement in mood. This surprised Laverne and, in fact, as her mood picked up, she found that the new routine of maintaining a reasonable diet became less problematic.*

Why alcohol and drugs can cause problems

Risks when well

Many people with a diagnosis of bipolar disorder will have used alcohol or other drugs at some time in the course of the illness. Alcohol can be very seductive if you are living with the changing mood states that can be part of bipolar disorder. One person described alcohol as having two different effects, namely to mask the effects of depression and to intensify the feeling of high spirits when mood was becoming elated. This person therefore found it hard to manage her intake of alcohol as there always appeared to be a reason for consuming it, whichever mood state she was experiencing. The problem with alcohol is that it has two effects. The first of these is that when small amounts of alcohol are consumed, when mood appears to improve, people often feel more relaxed and are able to socialise more easily. This is the most immediate effect of alcohol and is therefore the one that people are often most aware of; it is often, therefore, the effect that people, with or without bipolar disorder, seek when drinking. The secondary effect of alcohol is less immediately noticeable but is more important in the long term. This is its depressant effect. Most people who have had 'one too many' the night before will be aware the next day of feeling dehydrated and possibly a little lower in mood and more irritable than usual. However, even without drinking to excess, regular drinking often leads to a gradual deterioration in mood. Because this can be gradual, the connection with drinking may not be obvious at first. In fact, it is not uncommon for people to react to this decline in mood by drinking more to try to recapture the original effect of enhanced mood. This can then make the problem worse and there is a risk of developing a depressive episode.

Illegal drugs can also be used by people with bipolar disorder. Sometimes, this can again be to enhance already elevated mood, but often it can be an attempt to deal with depression. The risks of illegal drugs are high for various reasons:

1. Many drugs can exacerbate the mood problems associated with bipolar disorder.
2. Often unknown constituents of the drug being bought.
3. Possible criminal conviction and the additional burden of dealing with the consequences of this on top of bipolar disorder.

Stimulants such as amphetamine and cocaine can enhance mood in the short term, but their regular use is associated with a greater risk of relapse in people with bipolar disorder. Similarly, other drugs such as cannabis, which are taken for their predominantly calming effects, have been associated in sensitive individuals with increases in symptoms. For these and the above reasons, it is recommended that illegal drugs be avoided.

In addition to the chemical effects that alcohol and illegal drugs can have, their use can also interfere with mood because of their effects on how people behave. For instance, alcohol is associated with poorer quality of sleep and thus with greater feelings of tiredness and fatigue. When alcohol is taken in large quantities, regular sleep can be badly affected, diet can deteriorate and it can be difficult or impossible to commit to your regular activities. These changes can in themselves be associated with mood changes in people with bipolar disorder and thus with risk of further illness. The following provides an example of the build-up of negative effects that stimulants can have.

case

When Donald left home for university, he began to experiment with alcohol and cannabis. This was partly because he was quite shy and felt that the combination of these two drugs made him more confident and sociable. However, whereas at first he used both on an occasional basis, he soon began to use them daily and in increasing amounts. As he used more alcohol, he began to sleep more erratically and began to become at times quite threatening after an evening of drinking. This would cause him problems the following day as he felt ashamed and embarrassed after the previous night's behaviour, which, when he was not drinking, was completely out of character. To deal with these feelings he would feel drawn to drink again and hence the problems would continue. As his mood problems mounted, the pattern of drinking probably combined with his developing elevated mood and caused increasing chaos in his daily life. Over subsequent years, Donald had further periods of problem drinking, although he didn't use cannabis again. However, at the time of working with his current therapist, he had made a decision to avoid alcohol altogether because, although he had never become addicted to it, the pattern of problematic use and associated mood difficulties had become very apparent to him.

It is important to emphasise here that we are not suggesting that nobody with a diagnosis of this type should ever drink. This is clearly unrealistic, and many people with bipolar disorder are able to drink in a controlled fashion. As stated in the previous chapters, it is important that you control the situation. If you can enjoy a drink in moderation, then all's well and good. It is, however, useful to note from time to time how much you are drinking in order to be alert to any increases in consumption so that it does not start to control you through triggering changes in mood and behaviour.

Risks when unwell

Especially when mood is high, there can be additional risks that drugs or alcohol may be used 'out of character'. Some people have described experimenting with street drugs when entering a manic phase, which they would not have contemplated when their mood had been within normal limits. Similarly, alcohol consumption can increase rapidly with increased mood in some people. As mood is elevated, there can be a belief than no harm can come of drinking to excess and that you, unlike other people, can cope with it without ill effects. Of course, in reality we are all human and the depressant effects of excessive alcohol consumption can eventually have their impact in a crash into severe depression.

In the end, any decisions about alcohol and drug consumption are made by you as an individual. It is therefore important that these are made on the basis of good information. It can be useful to spend a little time thinking about how you have dealt with alcohol and drugs in the past. In doing this, it is best not only to rely on your own memory but also to check with people you trust, such as relatives or close friends. Use this information and your own memories to think through the good and bad things associated with alcohol or (if you have used them) drug use. Include the short term benefits if you had these, but do not forget to include problems possibly generated over a longer period.

If you decide to drink a lot because you enjoy it and there is no evidence of this having caused you any problems to date, then that is your choice – although in the long run it is one that is likely to be associated with health problems. If, however, your thinking that you enjoy it is based only on the short-term effects and ignores the role heavy drinking may have played in episodes of illness, relationship problems, or job or financial difficulties, then your decision to continue drinking in this way is not based on all the available evidence and the cognitive-behavioural approach that we endorse would suggest that this should be revised.

Different types of relaxation

Different forms of relaxation can be useful in looking after yourself. This, again, is an issue that applies to everyone irrespective of whether or not they may happen to have a psychiatric diagnosis. However, it is again likely that employing relaxation as part of a balanced routine is associated with maintaining your psychological health. Formal relaxation techniques will be discussed in the following chapter and can be very useful. It is important, however, that relaxation is not just seen as a particular technique that is learned as a part of treatment. Relaxation means anything that is relaxing, and often this can be something that we don't notice unless we stop to think. Some relaxing activities that were brainstormed in a recent group discussion with people who were current users of mental-health services included:

- reading a good book
- going for a walk
- cycling
- watching a good film
- having a meal
- talking with friends
- laughing at a joke
- going to the gym
- standing still and looking at the view
- stroking a pet cat or dog
- listening to music

All of these can be useful, but everyone is different in what he or she feels is relaxing. So for some people watching TV would be irritating but going to the gym would be helpful. Other people might be allergic to pets but love reading. It is therefore a case of finding which combination of activities suits you. This is the easy bit! The hard part is then making sure that you do them on a regular basis. Relaxing activities do not have to take up large amounts of time, but they do have to occur reasonably frequently within your week if you are to feel the benefits of them. It can be useful to post reminders to yourself in a diary or on a board in the kitchen to prompt you to remember these activities when other things are threatening to demand all of your time.

Safe thrills

Living with bipolar disorder in a way that optimises your mental health involves avoiding activities and behaviours that you know from experience have been associated with previous mental-health problems. This does not, however, mean that all stress must be avoided, or that any form of excitement is off limits. Indeed, one of the key advantages of having a reasonable routine is that it is possible to think ahead and plan in 'safe thrills'. These are activities that are exciting and engaging without being associated with health risks. They may include:

- climbing
- swimming
- watersports
- travel
- computer games
- flying/racing simulation games
- jogging/running
- hiking

But again, as with relaxation, the key is to identify activities that have an element of excitement but are not associated with risks to your health (in contrast to using alcohol or drugs, working excessively hard or taking risks with your finances by over-spending).

POINTS COVERED IN THIS CHAPTER

1. Having a reasonable routine is important in staying healthy, but this does not mean having to do exactly the same things every day.
2. What you eat is important because of the impact physical health has on mental well-being. Also, making the effort to eat well sends an important message to you that you are worth that effort.
3. Drugs and alcohol are particularly risky if you have bipolar disorder. They are sometimes used to mask depression and also to fuel mania. Illegal drugs should be avoided. Many people with bipolar disorder manage to drink in moderation when well, but it is important to be aware of the risks of abuse when moods change.
4. Relaxation is important for everyone. The challenge is to find a number of activities that are relaxing for you. This will vary from person to person.
5. It is sometimes helpful to look for other activities or interests that provide 'safe thrills' so as to avoid boredom setting in and more risky behaviour developing from this.

Chapter 7

Vicious cycles and how to deal with them

This book was written on a computer, which allows us to offer a personal example of the chapter topic: the role of vicious cycles in causing psychological problems. The particular vicious cycle we refer to is set up by the easy availability of computer Solitaire when one is writing. The trigger is stress: you have many things to do and are aware of the lack of time in which to do them. You may also feel worried or unsure about what you are writing: What if it's not good enough? A natural reaction is to say, 'OK, I'll play a couple of games of Solitaire and that will relax me.' A half-hour later you realise that a half-hour has been wasted, leaving less time to deal with multiple demands. The danger is that you are now more stressed and feel the need to play yet more Solitaire to relax.

Vicious cycles are often found to play an important role in a variety of psychological problems. You stop at the pub, vowing to have only a half-pint because you have important things to do later in the day. The first half-pint induces a pleasant sense of relaxation, followed by the thought, 'Wouldn't a pint taste nice about now?' and this may in turn lead to a day of excess drinking. Low mood and self-blame may follow, and for some people this will lead to more drinking and an escalating problem. Procrastination can commonly set up a vicious cycle; the more you delay in tackling problems and tasks, the more difficult they come to seem, and the more you want to postpone them further. Most important from the point of view of this book, both manic and depressive states can be exacerbated by vicious cycles, as can some of their symptoms, such as stress, anxiety and anger. This chapter looks at vicious cycles: how to understand them better and how to deal with them.

Vicious cycles and stress

As should be clear from the previous chapters, vicious cycles operate in both manic and depressed states. The manic person feels powerful, attractive and successful and believes that whatever he or she does will go right. Such thoughts can easily lead to excessive activity and loss of sleep, which in turn can exacerbate the manic episode. The depressed person, on the other hand, feels worthless, helpless and likely to fail. This can lead to inactivity and social isolation, which in turn can often make a depressed mood worse. In both cases, feelings are probably a bad guide to action. Thus, the manic person should avoid driving at 90 m.p.h. on the motorway although he *feels* sure that nothing bad will happen, while the depressed person should not stop going to work, even though she definitely doesn't *feel* like it. Neither of these things is easy to do; all people naturally act on the way they feel, and often feelings do provide a very good guide to action. However, if you can recognise that you are in a vicious cycle, especially one you have experienced before, this is the first step to breaking out of it.

These ideas naturally follow from those discussed in previous chapters. The cognitive strategies discussed in chapter 4 give you ways of stepping back from unhelpful thoughts rather than being carried along with them. One of the benefits of routine, as discussed in chapter 6, is that it anchors you against sudden impulsive actions that might be unhelpful.

Paying attention to vicious cycles is also important in dealing with stress, which is in itself a very important topic, not only for bipolar sufferers but also for most people today. The high level of stress in our society is especially relevant to bipolar sufferers because, as chapter 1 explains, stress can sometimes play a part in triggering episodes of mania, hypomania or depression. Stress is defined in two ways: it can refer to a situation that puts a large number of difficult demands on us, and it can also refer to the feelings that such situations generate. Modern life is stressful in general because people feel that there are so many things they have to deal with, so many demands and obligations, and seemingly, for many people, less and less time to deal with them. A certain amount of stress can be helpful: it pushes us to do new things, and overcoming it can create a sense of accomplishment. Excessive stress, however, can lead to a four-stage vicious cycle:

1. You are faced with multiple demands, some of which seem difficult, frightening or unpleasant. You think about what you will need to do to meet these demands, and this seems impossible or very unpleasant.
2. You feel anxious, tense and on edge. You become preoccupied with worries and mental images of the difficulties and problems facing you.
3. You do things that make you feel better. These might range from the computer Solitaire discussed earlier in this chapter to various other forms of procrastination and avoidance (e.g. watching lots of television, washing the kitchen floor), and on to activities, such as excessive use of alcohol or recreational drugs, that can cause long-term harm.
4. The demands remain unmet and the problem unsolved, thus leading to more worry and preoccupation.

We are sure that most of you have experienced this pattern in some form: all of the authors certainly have! The first step in managing stress is generally through the use of diaries and lists. As you may have noted in previous chapters, cognitive-behavioural therapy approaches rely to a large extent on the client putting his or her thoughts, worries and concerns on paper; this is in part because such a procedure forces you to think about them in a different, more objective, way. The use of lists and diaries also allows you to prioritise your various obligations. Lists are useful because they encourage you to tackle your various obligations in a systematic way; as you begin to check them off, you realise that it feels better to tackle problems than to run away from them. By using a diary or appointment book, one can also allot times to deal with specific problems and tasks.

Two other suggestions are important. First, if you see that there are simply too many problems to be tackled in a period of time, then some of them have to be postponed, given to someone else to deal with, or simply not done. The use of lists and schedules allows you to decide which tasks those should be, rather than having something remain undone by default. Second, by looking at a list of your problems and tasks, you can pick out those for which you need more information. With many things it is helpful to seek advice, either from a professional or from a friend or partner. If there is someone you can trust to help you with a particular problem, use him or her! Remember that no one is so wise or expert that they know the answer to all of life's problems. The following example shows how Melissa uses diaries to manage her stress.

case | *Melissa has learnt over the last few years that the use of diaries and time-management strategies are very important in managing her illness. When she is low she will avoid doing things. She has learnt that booking things to do in her diary helps her to keep active. On the other hand, when she is high she will be very open and enthusiastic about new ideas and projects. As a result, she often commits herself to too many projects at once and becomes stressed and anxious. She has now learnt never to take on a project that she cannot fit in her diary, and this strategy helps her to resist the temptation to over-commit herself.*

Problem solving

So called 'problem solving therapy' has a long history; it is well established in cognitive-behavioural therapy, but a similar approach is used in a variety of fields ranging from business management to military strategy. It is basically a common-sense approach to dealing with problems and difficulties and involves three steps:

1. Define the problem and the desired outcome. Laverne, for example, defined one problem as the way she tended to pass her evenings: she would often spend hours in front of the television watching programmes she didn't really enjoy because she felt too tired to do anything else. In therapy, she was able to define the problem as: 'finding a way to spend my evening that will be relaxing without making me feel that I've wasted my time'. Defining the problem helped her to rule out certain approaches that would not have been helpful, such as looking for a second job or doing vigorous physical exercise. Having defined the problem, you then move on to:

2. Considering possible solutions. At this stage, the key is to practise what is called 'brainstorming', that is, looking at all possible solutions, no matter how far-fetched some of them may seem at first glance. The idea of this rule is to free the mind to think as creatively as possible. Laverne considered a variety of courses, hobbies and projects, ranging from painting her flat and studying a foreign language to needlepoint and watching videos of nature programmes. At this stage of the process, it is also useful to solicit a variety of opinions and suggestions from a number of people. It may also be helpful to take several days for this part of the process, writing down possible solutions as they occur.

3. Eliminate the less sensible solutions, choose one of those that remain, and try it out. Laverne finally decided on a variety of activities: she decided to take an evening class in English Literature, as that would also give her reading to do, and she

also decided to take up knitting, which she had learnt when she was young. Knitting seemed like a good idea for her because she found it relaxing, and also because she could give away the clothes she knitted as Christmas presents.

As with scheduling, problem solving often works best if the problem and possible solutions are written down. It offers a simple and practical approach to looking for solutions to a variety of problems. It also offers an alternative to simply worrying about some problem by presenting a systematic way of attacking it.

Relaxation

Another problem caused by stress is the unpleasant bodily feelings and thoughts that it can create. These include sweating, agitation, restlessness, rapid heartbeat, stomach problems, etc. In extreme cases, these symptoms can result in a panic attack, especially when a person believes that they are the sign of some underlying physical problem. They are generally not; they are normal symptoms of anxiety, which almost everyone experiences, but they can still be very unpleasant. In addition, anxiety causes changes in the way we think: the anxious person experiences dangers as magnified, threats as more likely and more unpleasant than they really are, and unlikely events as highly likely. This is natural, but it can lead to excessive worry about relatively unlikely events. Finally, worry can interfere with sleep. For all these reasons, a method of reducing anxiety can be very useful.

Throughout her daughter's childhood, Laverne experienced frequent intrusive worries about her welfare. She worried that her daughter was unhappy at school, that she would do poorly in her studies, that she was being bullied, and that her life would be unhappy. These worries were combined with intense guilt. Laverne felt that if her daughter did badly in life, it would be her fault because she was a bad mother. These worries sometimes kept Laverne awake at night. Fortunately, a friend suggested that she listen to late-night talk radio programmes. Laverne found this helpful because the discussions would sometimes distract her from her worries and help her to fall back to sleep.

This example illustrates how distressing and unpleasant many intrusive worries can be. It is useful to distinguish between useful and useless worries. A useful worry concerns something you can do something about: remembering to pay bills on time or do a necessary household task. In this case, worrying can sometimes lead to a useful idea or solution for your problem. Useless worries are ones that centre on something you can do nothing about. Laverne's worries about her daughter could not help her daughter to do better in school. Relaxation techniques can be helpful in dealing with such useless worries.

With this in mind, we would like to offer a few simple relaxation techniques. The basic idea of relaxation training is to set aside time to relax. The main necessities are a quiet room, a comfortable chair and half an hour of time when there will be no interruptions. The aim is to sit quietly, clear your mind of worries and concerns, enjoy the relaxed state and come to recognise how it feels. A variety of techniques can be used:

1. *Deep breathing.* Practise counting to three slowly, allowing about a second between each count. Then breathe in through your nose to the count of three, and out through your mouth to the same count. Try to concentrate on your breathing and notice how it feels. Breathing is particularly useful because it is something you can do almost anywhere. It involves no special equipment and is inconspicuous, so it can be done in a public place.

2. *Repeating a phrase.* Chanting or repeating prayers or phrases is an ancient and well-established way of putting your mind into a relaxed and contemplative state. Buddhists practise chanting for religious purposes and Catholics say their Hail Marys using a rosary. The repeating of some soothing phrase,

either out loud or silently, is a well-established form of meditation. For those not religiously inclined, a phrase like 'Peace' or 'Relax', repeated over and over again, can often induce a calm state of mind.

3. *Listening to soothing music.* A variety of types of music has been suggested for this purpose. Some suggest soothing baroque or classical music: Pachelbel's Canon is a popular example, and CD collections of classical favourites are widely available. Gregorian chanting has also been suggested. For those who prefer, either popular music or jazz works just as well, providing the works chosen are soothing and mellow. Many record shops sell CDs specifically marketed as 'for relaxation', containing, for example, birdsong or the sound of waves breaking. A bit of trial and error can be useful here: you need to try various types of music and find out what works best for you.

4. *Deep muscle relaxation.* This method has been long used by clinical psychologists to teach anxious patients to relax. It involves tensing and relaxing all the muscle groups in turn, and focusing one's attention on how muscles feel when they are tense, and how they feel when they are relaxed. The procedure takes about twenty minutes. One useful aid is to put the script onto an audiotape and listen to it. Appendix B contains instructions and a full transcript.

All these methods work partly through distraction: chanting, breathing and music occupy the mind, making it easier to exclude worrying thoughts. This is why Laverne found listening to the radio so helpful. They also work by teaching you what it feels like to be relaxed; as you learn to recognise the feeling of relaxation, you can learn how to recreate it at will.

Whatever method you find most helpful, we urge you to give it a trial of a couple of weeks to see how well it works and become adept at it. You should eventually find that you do not need the tape or CD to make it work: the goal is to be able to relax in a variety of circumstances, for example when waiting in a queue or in a doctor's waiting room, by rehearsing the method mentally. It is often useful to use a cue word, like 'Relax' when practising relaxation. This word can then be repeated to oneself as an aid to rapid relaxation. One use of such rapid relaxation is illustrated in the next section, on anger management.

One further point is very important. The experience of anxiety is generally not harmful, and in fact constitutes a normal part of human life. It is therefore very important not to become anxious about your anxiety, as this can compound the problem. Similarly, relaxation should be approached as something pleasurable, and you should not worry about whether or not you are 'doing it right'. We hope that you will look on the above strategies as suggestions and try them out to see which is best for you.

Anger and anger management

case

Imagine you are travelling by bus to a social engagement. You have waited a little too long to leave home and, as a result, you are very worried about being late. As the bus crawls through traffic, you find yourself growing tense and angry. Why is the bus moving so slowly? Why are the drivers in the surrounding traffic being so hesitant? Why are elderly passengers taking so long to board; don't they realise that other passengers might be in a hurry? As these thoughts run through your mind, you become angrier and angrier. You tap your fingers, look at your watch and squirm about in your seat. When you finally arrive, you are in a terrible mood and don't really enjoy the evening.

The above vignette provides, we hope, a good example of negative thinking in anger. Anger provides an excellent example of the vicious cycle phenomenon at work. It can be sparked by some situational trigger but can then also become self-feeding. This is because the angry person, as in the vignette above, generally feels that other people are behaving badly and that their angry feelings are justified. As you become angrier, your angry thoughts often become more extreme, and more and more reasons to be angry form in your mind. A good example of this can be found in arguments that occur in a marriage or relationship: the partners, as they argue, think of all sorts of reasons to be angry at one another. "Do you remember that time, seven years ago, when I wanted to go to the beach and you didn't?' Even when the experience of anger is very unpleasant, we often find it hard to give up because we feel that if we do, the other person will somehow have won.

Anger can, of course, be a problem for a variety of people, but some people with bipolar disorder can be especially troubled by it when they are high. Anger can be related to a sense of grandiosity: if you feel that you have special abilities and talents, then you will have little patience with others who want to stop you from doing things that you feel are perfectly reasonable. The fact that others see them as unreasonable, and in fact that you might see them as unreasonable in a different state of mind, seems to be irrelevant. This makes the subject of anger management particularly relevant for people with bipolar disorder.

The following example shows how Donald and his parents cope with Donald's anger.

case | *Even though Donald has, in general, a good relationship with his parents, there are times, especially when he is becoming elated, that he feels very angry with them. For example, when they ask him if he has taken his tablets, something they are likely to do when they see that he is becoming high, he can find this very irritating. 'What right have they to pry? I'm a man in my thirties; my parents shouldn't be checking up on me! Do they think I'm just a child? They're always too quick to criticise and find fault.' These thoughts can precipitate angry arguments. Fortunately, Donald and his parents have been able to discuss these clashes when he is in a more normal mental state, and Donald has also had the chance to ventilate genuine grievances and point out times when his parents have been intrusive.*

Anger-management techniques are difficult to apply, precisely because the angry person often does feel that his or her anger is justified. If you feel that you would benefit from some anger-management techniques, first look at the situations in which you get angry. Probably you will find that when you are angry, you will find yourself thinking about the bad behaviour of some other person or group of people, combined with the feeling that you are being attacked, humiliated or unfairly taken advantage of. Sometimes, as in the example at the beginning of this section, these thoughts will strike you, when you are calmer, as unfair and unreasonable. On the other hand, there may be a considerable amount of truth in these thoughts. Thus, Donald had some justification for his thoughts about his parents. Finally, if the thoughts are justified, you will need to decide whether or not you can express them to the offending party. Donald was able to talk to his parents, in an honest and assertive way, about how he felt about them, and all of them found this very helpful. On the other hand, there are some cases when this might not be possible. For example, if your boss is known to fire people who complain to him, even when their complaints are both reasonable and expressed in a reasonable manner, you may not be able to say anything to him. In such a case, you can either leave your job, or you can try to find ways to contain your anger. We will talk first about anger management and move on to assertiveness in the next section.

The first step in anger management is to use the methods of relaxation described in the last section. The old folk wisdom that the first thing to do when angry is to count to ten has a lot of truth in it. When you are angry, the immediate impulse is to strike out, either in words or actions, to wound the object of your anger. A well-practised relaxation routine, triggered by a well-rehearsed cue word, should be used as soon as you feel anger building up. It is also useful to prepare a group of 'coping self-statements', sentences you can say to yourself in an anger situation. Typical sentences could include, 'Let me be calm'. 'Let me think this out'. 'Work out what to do before you act.' Practise these sentences to yourself, especially before entering a situation you know might make you angry. The goal here is not to swallow your anger but to work out how best to express it.

As noted above, the key question is: 'Will expressing my anger be helpful in this situation?' Try to work out what is the best step for you to take. If you are in a situation in which you don't feel you can express anger directly, it is often useful to express it in another forum, perhaps talking about why you are angry and why you cannot express it directly with a trusted friend or partner. It can also be useful to write a letter to the person you are angry at, even if you do not send it. You may also want to think about how to avoid being in that situation in the future. Thus, as noted above, a job that produces many episodes of anger might be a job that you should think about leaving. The following example shows how Melissa deals with her anger at work.

case | *Melissa was often troubled by episodes of anger that accompanied changes in her mood. One result of this pattern was a number of rows with people at her work. These would often be about unimportant things: one very unpleasant argument with a colleague was triggered by his leaving a few papers on her desk. Melissa now has a rule for herself: whenever she is angry, she tells herself not to act in haste. One trick she uses is to go to the toilet to compose herself and think about the situation and what she should do about it. She has found that this way she can decide whether a matter is worth pursuing. If it is, she has also found assertive techniques helpful.*

Assertiveness

The term 'assertiveness' is often thought to refer to rudeness, pushiness and being self-important. Actually, the term refers to being able to express yourself and make your needs clear without being either pushy or aggressive. The assertive approach can be contrasted with the passive and aggressive ways of tackling a problem. The three approaches are exemplified below.

> *You buy a shirt in a shop. When you get it home, you find that one of the seams is badly sewn. The passive approach is to say nothing: you can wear the shirt and ignore the problem or just use it for rags. The aggressive approach would be to get very angry at the poor quality of merchandise in the shop, go back, and yell at the shop assistant. An assertive approach would be to take one's receipt and the shirt, return to the shop, and ask in a calm manner for another one.*

This is a simple example, and most people don't have much difficulty in returning merchandise to shops. However, the same basic approach can be useful in a variety of situations. Here are a few basic pointers:

1. It is best to express your grievance as calmly as possible, focusing on the way in which the situation makes you feel. It is often not helpful to focus on criticising the other person, but instead to explain how the situation impacts on you. For example, if a friend lets you down, it might be better to say, 'I was really hurt by what you did', than, 'You are a selfish, inconsiderate slob.'

2. Try to focus on those particular aspects of the situation that are distressing, and on explaining them as clearly as possible. You want the other person to understand how you feel and what you think he or she could do to make the situation better.

3. Make sure to listen carefully to what the other person has to say. If possible, try putting what they say in your own words to make sure you understand it. "Let me make sure I understand this. You are saying ...' You can also restate your position in light of this understanding, so both of you understand what the difference between the two points of view is.

4. Remember that your goal in any situation is a solution that is fair to everyone. Thus, by stating your position clearly but also understanding the other person's, the two of you should be able to negotiate a compromise that is satisfactory to everyone.

5. If the situation cannot be resolved in this way, consider what other steps you might take. If a clerk refuses to exchange your shirt, you can complain to the manager or write a letter of complaint to the head office, or simply say that you will never use that shop again. If a friend won't apologise for some inconsiderate action, you may have to decide how important an apology is to you and whether or not it is worth losing a friendship over the issue.

The following is a continuation of Donald's story. This is how Donald and his parents were eventually able to manage Donald's anger:

case | *As noted above, Donald had a number of conflicts with his parents, which often occurred when he was high. When he was very high he was not usually able to resolve these conflicts, and they would often escalate into clashes. However, both he and his parents found that such clashes could sometimes be averted by having the three of them sit down and discuss their differences in a rational manner. Both of Donald's parents were willing to admit that sometimes they were excessively worried, and the family as a whole learned that it could arrive at reasonable compromises.*

This chapter has been a long one, covering a number of different subjects. Stress, time management, relaxation, anger and assertiveness are complex topics. Appendix A contains a number of suggestions for advice books dealing with many of these areas: we suggest you look here if you need some further help with a particular topic.

POINTS COVERED IN THIS CHAPTER

1. Vicious cycles operate throughout our lives. They usually involve dealing with a stressful situation in such a way that the situation becomes worse.
2. Almost everyone can see examples of vicious cycles throughout their lives. They lie at the root of a variety of psychological problems.
3. Vicious cycles can be seen in both mania and depression: allowing either a high or a depressed mood to dominate one's thoughts and actions can often exacerbate these mood states.
4. Vicious cycles often occur in response to stress. Stress can be dealt with by carefully monitoring your activities and limiting demands on your time and resources.
5. Stress can also be dealt with through practising relaxation. There is a variety of relaxation methods and you should experiment and find what works best for you.
6. Anger often involves vicious cycles, as angry people often focus on thoughts that make them more angry.
7. Relaxation and taking time before acting are essential in dealing with anger.
8. It is often useful to write a letter to the person you are angry with to help in composing your thoughts.
9. When possible, you should confront the person you are angry with and express your grievance in an assertive way, while looking for a solution that both you and the other person can live with.

Chapter 8

The risks of sleep loss

Everyone needs sleep. It is during sleep that the body recharges itself both physically and psychologically. However, although it is known to be important, there is no fixed dose of sleep that is necessary for all people. You may recall the famous claim made by Margaret Thatcher that during her years as Prime Minister of Great Britain she required only 3–4 hours' sleep per night. Other people less famous (or infamous) report requiring widely differing amounts of sleep, from similarly brief periods right up to 10–11 hours. Sleep is an important issue for you if you have psychological problems. It can be disrupted by a wide of range of forms of psychological distress. If you have anxiety, stress or worry, you may find that your sleep is interrupted and shorter than usual, whereas if you are depressed, there may be times when you sleep for excessively long periods of time. The importance of sleep is emphasised in this chapter because it can serve either to help or to hinder the ways in which you deal with bipolar disorder.

The body clock

Sleep is especially important if you have bipolar disorder. The reasons for this are made clearer by considering the body clock, which we all possess.

There are natural changes in our bodily functioning that happen over a period of approximately 24 hours. These changes can be seen in alterations in body temperature, alertness, heart rate and rates of production of hormones and brain chemicals, amongst many other things. The technical term for these repeated changes that happen over a 24-hour period is 'circadian rhythm'. The body clock gives us important clues about when to be awake and asleep, when to eat, when to rest. When internal bodily signals (circadian rhythms) are in tune with the signals given by the outside world (lightness and darkness; other people's behaviour; periods of work and rest) then your systems work smoothly and you feel 'normal'. There are, however, many ways in which the body clock can be disrupted. If you regularly travel across time zones or do shift work then you may have experienced common symptoms such as fatigue and dysphoria. These are associated with a disruption of the connections between the information your body is giving you and the demands of your environment. Usually we can adjust to this with few problems and indeed people on long-term shift work can have similar problems readjusting if they take up more regular work patterns. However, if extreme and persistent changes occur in the environment then there can be long-term disruption to the body clock, which can have a significant impact on psychological health.

The body clock's association with mania and depression

It seems that if you have a bipolar or unipolar disorder, you may be more sensitive to disruptions of the body clock. Studies that have compared the operation of body clocks of people with bipolar disorder and people without such a diagnosis have tended to find differing patterns under 'normal' everyday conditions. Also, when there are situations when the operation of the body clock is disrupted, such as long plane journeys or working excessively long hours and missing sleep, it appears that the risk of mood problems increases. When such disruptions are particularly severe, it seems that the risk of these changes being of a manic type escalates.

There are situations in which circumstances beyond your control can cause disruption of the body clock. There are also times when your behaviour may make this disruption worse, usually without your intending to. An obvious example is if your mood is becoming high. When you feel in high spirits, interested in everything that is around you and positive about a wide range of tasks and challenges, then there will be a tendency not to want to waste time. This could lead you to work longer and longer hours and have less and less sleep or leisure time, buoyed up by your mood and feeling that you are making rapid progress. This can be experienced, for a period at least, as extremely positive and creative. The problem, however, is that this can then be associated with a later period when the disruption of normal routines leads to disruption of the body clock. This can then lead to further mood changes and eventually, if unchecked, to periods of 'restless hyperactivity'. These are periods when your mood is anxious, irritable and impatient rather than positive and optimistic. Furthermore, whereas previously it may have been possible to work productively on several projects at once, it is now difficult to concentrate on any particular task and thus you may find yourself moving from one task to the next, getting little done on each. In the early productive phase, sleep will be reduced because your time is taken up with more important things; however, when moving into this phase of restless hyperactivity, sleep is difficult because restlessness prevents it, as the following example illustrates.

case | *Donald described the early stages of his first period of mania, which began when he was at college. As noted in chapter 1, Donald began to become more outgoing and started experimenting with drugs and alcohol. During this time, his sleep pattern got less regular and the amount of sleep he was having reduced. His body clock was therefore affected by both the reduced quantity and reduced regularity of sleep. It is likely that these changes would have affected his body clock and that this would 'feed in' to his developing mood problem. As he pursued his creative interests with more and more vigour and became less aware of his routine needs for sleep and other important activities, the disruption in his body clock would have become increasingly severe. In this situation, therefore, Donald's behaviour following his initial mood change probably increased the impact of the original change and moved him more rapidly towards the manic state that he finally found himself in.*

In the early stages of depression you may have a different experience. Here there might be a tendency to want to withdraw. As mood becomes lower, the world can seem to be a more hostile place. Tasks that were previously challenging and positive can feel like overwhelming problems. Minor relationship difficulties can feel as though they are evidence of likely abandonment. Previously interesting and engaging hobbies and pastimes can seem pointless and irritating. In the context of these situations, it can be understandable that hiding away can seem like a reasonable option. This could either be the result of a conscious decision or a reaction to feeling an increased need for longer and longer periods of sleep. This situation can again interfere with your body clock. This disruption can be associated with feelings of fatigue and further low mood, which can then make the original problem worse. So the early stages of low mood may have been triggered by a milder body-clock disruption, or by natural fluctuation in mood, but then how you respond to these early changes could affect whether they get worse or better. The following extract shows how Melissa responded to such changes.

Melissa is aware that her mood seems to fluctuate for a number of reasons. One important factor for her seems to be the time of year. She says that her mood is low during winter months in particular. On several occasions she has required additional treatment for depression at this time of year. She often notices her mood beginning to decline in late autumn and as it does, she feels less energetic, less interested in things and more tired. Her job often involves periods of intense activity, finishing off particular contracts for tight deadlines. During a low period she will often struggle to keep up with any additional work demands and says that sometimes she will 'hide'. For Melissa, hiding means staying away from work for several days and doing little else but sleeping and watching TV. She lives alone and is therefore quite isolated during these periods. Sometimes she can then get herself back into the swing of things and beat the low. However, last year this didn't happen. A few days turned into a few weeks and a few extra hours turned into 16–18 hours' sleep per day. As her body clock changed, feelings of lethargy, depression and hopelessness increased. Eventually, Melissa was visited by her mother, who, alarmed by her daughter's situation, contacted her doctor, which led eventually to Melissa agreeing to a hospital admission.

The importance of checking your own mood

The above account might look rather bleak. At first glance, it might seem that these escalating changes can never be under your control and that recurrent periods of worsening or elevating mood are inevitable. However, the picture is more positive than that. We have found, from the clients we have worked with, that you can become extremely skilled at monitoring fluctuations in your mood. As a result of this, you can be alert to early mood changes, whether these are caused by disruption of your body clock or by other events. When alerted to such changes, one of the courses of action that can be taken is to act to reduce their impact. In the case of elevating mood, people with bipolar disorder have described to us how they used to give up on sleep at an early stage because they wanted to get on with other things. However, if they identified this change at an early stage, sleep was often still possible, albeit sometimes taking rather longer to achieve. By persisting, people were often then able to 'ride out' the mood change without it escalating into an unpleasant period of restless hyperactivity or 'crashing' into profound depression, as in the example of Donald below. (These issues are also considered in the description of early warnings in chapter 5.)

case | *Donald has learnt skills for monitoring his own mood through his work with a clinical psychologist. He now has a rating scale, which he keeps in his diary. He makes a simple −10 to +10 mood rating every day, even when things seem fine. As a result of doing this, in conjunction with other strategies described elsewhere in this volume, he has been able cope with periods when his mood has begun to show signs of going 'high'. In particular, it seems for Donald that if he is rating himself +6 for more than a couple of days, this can be a sign of impending trouble. When he notices this, he then uses his coping skills to maintain his body-clock routines, among other things, and has so far been successful in increasing his feeling of control over changes in mood rather than feeling at their mercy, as he did previously.*

The problem with caffeine

Virtually everyone drinks some drinks that contain caffeine. The obvious drinks that have this stimulant are coffee and tea. It is also contained in many soft drinks, especially energy drinks and cola, as well as in a range of widely available medications such as cold remedies. Caffeine acts as a stimulant, which means that initially it seems to increase alertness and reduce feelings of fatigue. However, when taken in high doses it appears to have a significant impact on sleep. People who consume caffeine in the hour before going to bed will often be delayed in going to sleep compared with those who have not done so. Also, once asleep, people who have consumed more than four or five cups of coffee in a day may tend to have greater problems in staying asleep, even if the caffeine is not taken within the hour before bed. Once asleep, the quality and duration of sleep can also be impaired by the caffeine use on the previous day.

Since sleep is important in relation to the functioning of the body clock, and particularly in people with bipolar disorder, it is wise to be alert to caffeine consumption. It is unlikely that caffeine consumed at the level of two or three cups per day would cause significant problems, but above this level there might begin to be effects on sleep. Clearly, as with all the issues discussed in this book, there is a great deal of variability between people in their reactions to caffeine, so it is important to get a clear idea of its effects on you as an individual. It is also worthwhile checking out which drinks contain caffeine if you are trying to cut down, or else you may inadvertently switch from one source of the stimulant to another (i.e. from coffee to tea or caffeinated soft drinks). Keeping a record of your consumption of caffeine-containing drinks and medications over a period of a week or so can often be a useful way of getting an idea of how much caffeine you are consuming. Often there will be some surprises in the record, as most of us are not terribly accurate in our estimates if we do not write things down. If you are taking more than the equivalent of two to three cups of instant coffee per day (or roughly four to six cups of tea or cola drinks) then it would be worth considering reducing your intake to this level or below. If you do this, then keep a note of how well you are sleeping and how refreshed you feel after sleep for a period of 2–3 weeks to give you an indication of the impact this reduction of caffeine intake might be having for you.

Air travel and mood

The information above indicates that there are some risks attached to extended air travel for people with bipolar disorder. We do not see this as an indication that you should avoid all such travel, but rather that some caution and planning should be employed. An awareness of this vulnerability can lead to a protective action plan when foreign travel is coming up. Some people find that, with their doctor's approval, taking a small supply of sleeping tablets can be helpful in keying the body in to new sleep/wake routines after arrival in a different time zone. Planning to avoid intense work immediately on arrival can again be important in giving the system time to adjust before subjecting it to further pressure. It can also be useful to try to plan such trips so as to ensure they do not occur with excessive frequency over a short period of time, as this may have a knock-on effect. Our experience has been that you can become attuned to your individual tolerance limits for travel and jet lag – and as long as you work within these then few problems occur. Another factor to consider is your general physical health; travelling extensively when under the weather can be particularly unwise, as can significant use of alcohol, which might exacerbate jet lag.

POINTS COVERED IN THIS CHAPTER

1. Sleep is important for everyone and people differ in how much they need.
2. We all have a body clock that keep us in tune with the routines of daily life such as sleep times.
3. If the body clock is disrupted then this can trigger changes in mood.

4. People with bipolar disorder are generally sensitive to body-clock disruption.

5. Self-monitoring helps warn you when to take action to protect yourself from the consequences of initial disruption of the body clock.

6. Skilled self-monitoring helps maintain varied lifestyles whilst minimising the risk of mood problems occuring.

7. Caffeine can at higher doses cause sleep problems. Monitoring caffeine consumption and keeping it to a low level – two or three cups of instant coffee per day (or equivalent) – can help maintain sleep quality and duration.

8. Air travel can affect mood. Being alert to these changes and avoiding putting your system under undue pressure can be important in staying well.

Chapter 9

Family issues

Family and bipolar disorder

Our experience is that most sufferers of bipolar disorder manage to leave home and live fairly independently from their family of origin. Some sufferers have married or are in stable relationships. However, it does not always mean that their family of origin is not involved, particularly when the sufferer becomes ill. In this chapter we will discuss issues of family involvement and how families are affected by the illness, either from the perspective of families of origin or sufferers' own families.

Involvement of family of origin

As discussed in chapter 1, bipolar disorder or unipolar depression (depression without any manic or hypomanic episodes) can often run in families. Thus, parents can feel very guilty if they have a history of illness in their families and therefore feel responsible for passing the illness on. This can be particularly pertinent if the onset of the illness occurred when the sufferer was still living at home. One reaction to feeling guilty can be for parents to become involved in every aspect of care and sometimes to be very direct in giving advice to the sufferer.

Although parental support can be very welcome and indeed

sometimes necessary to help a person access appropriate care at the beginning of an illness, it can then be difficult to work out appropriate levels of involvement as the course of the bipolar disorder continues. Over-involvement can cause a lot of resentment in the sufferer, particularly when the sufferer perceives the over-involvement as an infringement of personal freedom. Sometimes, even though the individual has managed to leave home, parents may still find it hard to let go.

With younger adults, parents are often concerned about the sufferer's social competence in managing money and coping with friends. Sexuality is another issue. Parents often worry about the sufferer having unprotected casual sex with 'undesirable characters' and that this may lead to unwanted pregnancy and venereal disease, including AIDS. Even if these worries may not be articulated, sufferers are closely watched. We have also come across adult sufferers who have left home and yet they have contact with their parents almost daily and would not make any decision without consulting them. The over-vigilance and over-involvement may be counter-productive and cause a lot of friction in the family. In these circumstances, we normally encourage families to have open and honest discussions about each other's fears and concerns and to come up with solutions that are acceptable to all sides in order to foster mutual trust and respect. Often, with the optimal amount of mutual respect the sufferer is more able to ask for help appropriately. This process requires an understanding of the views of both people with bipolar disorder and their carers.

The risks outlined above are real ones that many parents worry about and it is understandable that these worries would be heightened by the knowledge that a child has a disorder that can at times have unpredictable effects on behaviour. However, people with bipolar disorder are at greater risk of becoming unwell in an atmosphere of family tension and often the signs of family tension can themselves be signs of illness in the person with bipolar disorder. It is therefore of great importance that a balance is drawn between the parental desire to protect from harm and the young adults' need to progess in their development as autonomous individuals.

The following case vignette is a conversation between a sufferer and her parents about their experience of the illness.

case

Melissa: *I am grateful for your concerns most of the time. However, sometimes I feel that I am doing things to please you and dad. I feel that I am older now and I should be able to make decisions more independently.*

Mother: *I understand what you mean. However, it is hard for us to let go as well. Your illness started when you were making your mark at university. It was such a serious breakdown. We had to collect you from university and look after you for several weeks. Even long afterwards, you sometimes still made irrational decisions.*

Melissa: *I know. However, I sometimes feel I am being watched every step. I am living with my partner now. And yet I often feel the need to consult you and dad.*

A review of past episodes of illness for Melissa indicated that quite clearly the family being vigilant and over-protective did not work. Her parents had tried that in the past and there were still relapses. In fact, at times, Melissa was resentful and rebelled against her parents. The family then proceeded to discuss what may be the sensible way to help Melissa whenever she needs it without being too intrusive. This became a constructive dialogue in which Melissa was able to acknowledge those aspects of family support that were beneficial as well as those that led to conflict. This meant that there was scope for compromise, which left the parents with an active and constructive role in supporting Melissa, but allowed Melissa herself to retain a feeling of autonomy.

Involvement of spouses and partners

Spouses and partners can be of great support, though they do often have their own feelings to cope with as well in living with someone with bipolar disorder. Some husbands or wives may have married their partner in the full knowledge that they suffered from bipolar disorder and have accepted that as 'part of the deal' in choosing to be with this particular person. However, it can often be the case that bipolar disorder becomes apparent after the relationship becomes established. This can mean a lot of grief and anger for both partners as they try to come to terms with both the life they had envisaged together and the changes wrought by the onset of enduring mental problems. Distress can be particularly acute if a partner enters into a relationship in ignorance of the other's bipolar disorder through not being informed of the ongoing illness by the person with bipolar disorder. Again, it can be important to respect the views of both partners in these situations to try to work towards a situation in which communications between partners serve to facilitate progress rather than perpetuate conflict. In addition, it is often the case that spouses without a mental health problem often do get very little support or information. This can lead to them struggling alone with difficult challenges and so experiencing significant emotional distress. Support for partners (as is discussed later in this chapter) is therefore often an important factor in reducing conflict within relationships.

Here is an example of how Jean suddenly realised that her husband was suffering from bipolar illness. She was talking in a research interview we were conducting about spouses' experiences.

case | Jean: *I had no idea that he was suffering from manic depression. I knew that he had been depressed before we got married and his mood could be up and down. But I never knew. Then one day I was painting the bathroom and I was listening to a programme on the radio about manic depression. The presenter described the symptoms of manic depression and I thought 'That's it. That's my husband.' It turned out that he had been secretly going to the psychiatrist and having treatment for it.*

When relationships within the family are positive, there is great potential there for support for people with bipolar disorder. Some people voluntarily surrender their credit card to their spouses when they feel their mood elevating to keep until they no longer feel high. Power of attorney can also be given to the spouse so that the spouse can be entrusted to take the correct action to prevent financial and career ruin. However, families are different. Power of attorney can be a sensitive issue. It is not recommended for every family. Any powers or agreements within the family that could be seen to be restrictive by the person with bipolar disorder need to be treated with caution. It is extremely important that prior consent is given when the person with bipolar disorder is not in a period of mania or severe depression and that the terms under which such restrictions might operate are clear and agreed by both sides. If this type of approach is agreed in these circumstances, with the sufferer fully aware of the role that these restrictions might play in avoiding significant harm, it can work very well. If, however, the restrictions are in some way imposed on the person with bipolar disorder in a way that does not make sense to the sufferer, then it may merely become a further source of difficulty and tension.

Family members can have a vital role in helping sufferers to notice early signs of relapse so that they can use psychological skills to avert further problems or seek help from their mental-health team. However, a balance needs to drawn between this positive role and the risk of friction between family members if they are seen to be over-sensitive to even small changes in the behaviour of the person with bipolar disorder. This balance involves a recognition that all people experience fluctuating mood states, including anger, happiness, frustration, boredom and excitement. Thus, evidence of irritability in someone with a diagnosis of bipolar disorder is not necessarily a sign of anything more than their being irritated by an event in a normal way. When family members can communicate about these issues, they can pool their knowledge to identify those changes that are significant for the individual and those that are 'normal variation'.

Here is an example of how the sufferer and parents negotiate what they should do if there are signs of relapse.

Donald: *It is not helpful for you to say that I ought to see a doctor all the time. That really irritates me.*

Father: *It is exactly that. Whenever you become ill we notice that you are irritable with us and you are impossible to reason with.*

Donald: *Sometimes I get irritated for a good reason. You are irritable at the best of times. Why don't you see a doctor?*

I spoke to my therapist and he was pleased that you have commented on the list of early warnings. He suggested that we make time to talk about how you can help with detecting early warnings and seek help appropriately. *

Father: *Only if you do not resent it.*

Donald: *Yes, as I said, it is irritating when you get asked to see the doctor at the drop of a hat.*

---

*Depending on the quality of the relationship, sometimes it is useful to help the family of sufferers to detect an episode and seek help early. However, much tact is needed to help the family to come to some agreement.

Father: *I will talk only if you do not throw yourself into a temper.*

Donald: *I will try not to if you talk calmly with me. Lack of sleep and phoning people a lot are clearly early warnings for a manic attack. Irritability on its own may not be an early warning.*

Father: *Yes but you are resentful if we say anything.*

Donald: *Only when you say 'You are ill again. Go and see the doctor.' I might not be ill.*

Father: *There you go. We are not allowed to say anything.*

Mother (who has been listening all the time): *Tell us what we are allowed to say.*

Donald: *You can say 'You have not been sleeping as much as usual and ring up people more than usual. Remember what happened in the past? Do we need to think about whether you are getting into an early stage of the illness?'*

Dealing with family breakdown after illness and rebuilding relationships

Some people with bipolar disorder comment spontaneously that the experience of being high has caused damage to their relationships. Apart from being more irritable, part of the nature of being high is to be more expansive in mood, more distractible and more sociable. It is quite common that sufferers may spend an enormous sum of money when in a manic state and get into debt. Being distractible, they may not accomplish any tasks at work or at home and can lose jobs as a result. Contact with people can also become more rewarding than usual. Sufferers may become more flirtatious and have affairs outside their intimate relationship.

Equally, being depressed can cause problems, but of a different kind. People can become tearful and full of pessimism. They can also withdraw from others, including their family, and become much less active. All of these issues can cause problems. Whether the sufferers are hospitalised or not, it is almost impossible for them to continue with their day-to-day commitments during a period of moderate to severe depression.

In bipolar disorder, therefore, there are two types of problems than can afflict the sufferers and their families. Having to cope with the problems of both depression and mania can be harder to understand for carers and spouses than dealing with depression in isolation. Episodes can cause a lot of problems for the family. Some symptoms of both depression and mania can be perceived as malicious or intentional.

We normally advise a sufferer to rebuild his or her relationship when well. However, clinical professionals have a role here as well in helping families to be educated about the symptoms of the illness so that they do not perceive the sufferer's illness behaviour as being malicious or lazy. When the sufferer is well, we advise him or her to put in extra effort to work on the damaged relationship and mend any ill feelings. This will often be within the context of ongoing therapeutic work with the individual, who will be encouraged to invite his or her partner to therapy sessions. Work on communication skills is very important. Couples are encouraged to discuss each other's feelings about their experiences in order to help them to process the often conflicting and powerful emotions that both may have concerning previous illness episodes. They are also advised to engage in more activities that they both value, including gestures from both sides to show their appreciation of each other, to help build up the positive sides of their relationship.

At times, families can be particularly resentful if they perceive an episode as having been triggered by sufferer's stopping his or her mood stabilisers. This is a tricky issue as families can see their sick relative as being irresponsible. However, family education can come in handy here. Professionals should make it clear that sometimes it is hard to judge whether sufferers stopped taking medication and then relapsed or whether they were in an early stage of relapse when they stopped taking medication. However, some families are still resentful over the behaviour of the sufferers despite an explanation of the illness. In these circumstances, family meetings should be called for with professionals to facilitate a frank discussion of feelings. Particularly the meaning associated with being on long-term medication should be explored within the family.

Issues with children can be complicated. If the illness started later in life, the sufferer's children can have memories of what the sufferer is normally like and easily identify illness behaviour. This can also be the case if there are periods of relative psychological stability between episodes. However, it can be more difficult for children to differentiate illness behaviour from normal behaviour when the sufferer has few periods of stability. Here, the healthy spouse could play an important role in teaching the children about the illness. Support from extended families can be of tremendous help. If the children are old enough, we normally advise a frank discussion of the illness with them.

Support for families and partners

It is important that families and partners get support. However, such support is rarely available when the sufferer is ill and almost impossible when the sufferer is fairly stable. Furthermore, commitment to regular meetings may not be what the family wants. After all, it could be another obligation to fulfil. Voluntary organisations such as the Manic Depressive Fellowship in Britain or the Manic Depressive and Depressive Association in the United States provide newsletters and local meetings in many places. These local meetings are often open meetings with no prior commitment to attend regularly. Some families have found them helpful. There are also websites now that cater for both people with bipolar disorder and their relatives. A number of these are listed in Appendix A of this book, along with other useful addresses.

When the children are still young, it is often an added burden for one parent to have to look after the other in an episode whilst simultaneously fulfilling both the paternal and maternal role. Children can often be challenging when one of their parents is unwell. Often members of extended families and close friends step in to help. However, if this has not yet happened, the spouse should feel free to ask. If extended families and close friends are not available or cannot provide adequate support, the spouse should contact social services for practical support.

POINTS COVERED IN THIS CHAPTER

1. Families can understandably have a lot of concerns about sufferers. Family involvement can be helpful, but over-involvement can lead to significant conflict and tension.
2. The concerns for the sufferer and how the family copes with the illness should be discussed openly and an acceptable way of coping with the illness should be negotiated.
3. In addition to the family of origin, spouses and partners can be very helpful in detecting the early stages of illness and encourage seeking professional help.
4. Family members and partners can often help to limit the damage of the illness. However, the strategies should be negotiated carefully and it should be remembered that each family is different.
5. When the sufferer is out of an episode, it is advisable to work on repairing any damage to a close relationship that the episode(s) may have caused.

6. Children in the family can also be affected. If the children are old enough, it is important to discuss the illness openly and explain that certain behaviour is due to the illness.

7. Spouses or partners can come under additional strain in families with young children. Help from extended families and from social services should be sought.

8. Strain in the family can be a result of not understanding the illness. Psycho-education for the family is very important.

Chapter 10

Feeling bad about one's illness – guilt, shame and stigma

Illnesses, by their definition, cause distress and discomfort, including both physical pain and mental distress. Some illnesses, however, can cause an additional problem by affecting the way we feel about ourselves around other people. Some diseases, for example, might cause disfigurement, making the sufferer feel embarrassed around other people. Some diseases may cause shame: for example, a sexually transmitted disease may cause embarrassment for the sufferer because of the way it was caught. So-called 'mental illnesses' are a prime example of this phenomenon. Sufferers may feel ashamed or embarrassed to admit to their diagnoses because of the possible reactions of others. Sufferers may also have negative ideas about what it means to suffer from bipolar disorder, or a secret feeling of guilt or shame because of past behaviour attributable to their illness. This chapter will discuss some of these problems.

Stigma

Stigma is a term used to describe two things, a feeling of prejudice or dislike towards some group on the part of the general population, and the corresponding feeling of shame caused in that group by that prejudice. The stigmatisation of the mentally ill has been much studied over the past fifty years, and a number of findings are generally agreed upon. First of all, it is clear that the general public is not well informed about the symptoms, causes and treatments of mental illness, and a considerable amount of prejudice does exist. It is likely that most lay people, that is, people with no special knowledge of psychology or psychiatry, do not have a clear idea about the nature of bipolar disorder or of how it might differ from other mental illnesses, such as schizophrenia. It also seems that those who stigmatise the mentally ill often believe in a number of myths about mental illness. These myths are often vague and based on little factual information. Some of these are discussed below.

Mentally ill people are more dangerous than others. Many of the worries about the dangerousness of the mentally ill stem from fears about 'care in the community', combined with a small number of highly publicised murders committed by some mentally ill people. If one is the victim of a violent crime, it is far more likely to be carried out by a 'sane' person, who is much more likely to be a family member or acquaintance than a stranger. Official statistics show that incidents in which a person with a serious mental illness kills a stranger are very rare. The homeless mentally ill, who are often feared by the public, are much more likely to be the victims of crime than its perpetrators.

Mental illness is untreatable. Some lay people believe that the mentally ill are bound to go from bad to worse, and that the only sensible treatment for such people is to keep them locked away from the rest of society. With this may go the belief that psychiatric medications are nothing but sedatives designed to keep patients docile, a belief summarised in the phrase 'the liquid cosh'. With that comes an image of those of us who are mental-health professionals: we are either wacky psychoanalysts with goatees and an obsession with the early childhoods and sexual secrets of our patients, or mad pill-pushers whose goal is to keep our patients 'drugged up to the eyeballs'. There is also a cliché that we are 'as mad as our patients'. Of course, a certain percentage of mental-health workers have mental-health problems themselves; in this we are no different from any other occupation or profession. But the real harm in these beliefs is that they discourage needy people from seeking treatment.

The mentally ill have only themselves to blame. Few people would come out and actually voice this belief, but some evidence suggests that many lay people equate mental illness with free choice. The idea seems to be that physical illnesses have a bodily cause, while mental illnesses must have some sort of mental cause, and therefore have been in some sense chosen by the sufferer. Such a belief can only be seen as a sign of confused thinking. As we have made clear, most authorities today believe that some form of brain dysfunction is responsible for bipolar disorder, as well as most other forms of serious mental illness. Similarly, if factors such as a sufferer's culture or upbringing play a role in causing mental health problems, he or she cannot be responsible for these factors either. For this reason, it is illogical to blame sufferers for their illnesses. At the same time, psychological factors play a role in the course of bipolar illness, and this is also true of many physical illnesses, such as asthma or diabetes. Some authorities have even suggested that the course of some cancers can be affected by the patient's psychological state. One can learn through psychological approaches to manage a variety of illnesses, both physical and mental.

Although research does suggest that stigmatisation of mental illness exists, it also suggests that lay attitudes are complex. Many lay people believe that the mentally ill deserve more care and support than they in fact receive, and some evidence suggests that, as time passes, lay people are gaining more understanding of mental-illness sufferers. Research also shows that those who know sufferers have more enlightened attitudes, which suggests that people can learn to deal with those with mental illness in more compassionate ways.

Diagnosis

Issues about diagnosis may add to the sufferers' feeling of stigma.

The specific and important point here is that for bipolar disorder and most other mental illnesses, the same diagnosis may be applied to people with very different symptoms, problems and levels of functioning. We hope that the case examples in chapter 1 illustrate this. Psychiatric diagnoses can be very blurred, without sharp divisions between sufferer and non-sufferer. Thus, some people who would not be diagnosed with bipolar disorder may have strong fluctuations of mood, with low down periods alternating with bursts of good mood and productivity. Some people may have long and pronounced highs with brief lows, while for others, like Laverne, depression may be the main problem. High states may vary, with some patients experiencing elation and others irritability, and with a range of different symptoms and behaviours. Insight, the ability to realise when one is ill, is also very variable. Some patients reject the label of illness and never feel that they are ill at all, preferring another label, like 'gifted' or 'possessed'. For this reason, it is very hard to make any generalisation about those who suffer from bipolar disorder or, for that matter, any other kind of mental illness.

Putting it another way, a diagnosis is a label. The main effects of any illness lie in the particular symptoms you experience and the practical problems that they create. The bottom line is the impact on your own life. It is the job of professionals to help you to overcome the distress and disability of the illness, not to add to it, and a diagnosis is only a guide to possible helpful treatments that can be offered. Unfortunately, diagnosis can have a negative impact, especially if it demoralises the person it is given to. Fear of receiving a particular diagnosis can also discourage sufferers from seeking help. But patients can also fight the bad effects of labelling, and one job of psychological approaches is to help in this fight.

Effects of stigma

Stigma seems to affect sufferers in two ways: through their reactions to others and through their feelings about themselves.

Some sufferers worry about the reactions of others, fearing that they may not be accepted or that other people will think of them as 'mad'. Alternatively, some people are more affected by internal feelings of shame and worthlessness, the feeling that they are deeply flawed or have a terrible secret. Bruce Link, a sociologist who has done a number of studies of stigma and its effects, divides up possible responses to stigma into three types: *avoidance*, *concealment* and *education*.

1. Avoidance simply involves avoiding situations in which stigma might become an issue, for example not signing up for a course or applying for a job for fear of rejection. The problem with this approach is that the sufferer is often cut off from activities that might boost self-esteem or make life more pleasurable.
2. Concealment might also be called 'passing': the sufferer acts the part of a 'normal' person and keeps his or her problem secret. A problem can arise here if, during normal social interaction, the sufferer encounters others making ignorant or critical comments about 'crazy people'. In such a situation you can speak up and risk rejection or keep silent and possibly feel like a hypocrite.
3. Finally, the educational approach involves speaking out and trying to educate others about the reality of illness.

All these tactics may have problems; we would advocate a flexible approach, combining concealment and education. Concealment can also be described as reticence or modesty: no one is obliged to tell other people their personal business on all occasions. On the other hand, opportunities to speak out and be more forthright can be chosen based on the people and situation involved. The following is an account of how one patient dealt with her sense of stigma at work.

case

When at work, Melissa was troubled by the thought that her workmates did not know about her bipolar disorder; these thoughts tended to trouble her most when she was feeling low. At such times, she would feel like a hypocrite and believe that if her colleagues knew about her diagnosis, they would shun her. In therapy she had several discussions about how to resolve this problem. Ultimately, she decided that she did not have to share her diagnosis with people at work, but she did tell them that she had a course of psychological treatment to help with 'her excessive moodiness'. She also told colleagues that she thought they could profit from therapy too. She later told her therapist that this approach felt appropriate to her.

Inner feelings of stigmatisation can produce a sense of low self-worth; you may feel damaged or inferior in some way. Such a feeling can be combated in two ways. Careful thought about one's state is necessary. Of course bipolar disorder can be a disabling and distressing illness. In this it is similar to many other disabilities. Few people would choose to be blind or paralysed, but this does not mean that the disabled person is of less worth than others are. A humane society is one with opportunity for all, even those with problems or disabilities. Probably the best way of combating the sense of stigma is to first obtain all the help that you can, and then to work to make your life as fulfilled as possible. This may not be an easy task, and those who do not suffer with bipolar disorder are certainly not in the position to lecture to sufferers. Still, this book is based on the idea that there is much people can do to diminish the bad effects of bipolar illness and lead more fulfilled lives.

Anger and loss

Following on from the points above, some sufferers we have worked with were troubled by deep feelings of anger or loss about the effects of bipolar disorder on their lives. When you are the victim of a disabling illness, the thought, 'Why me?' is a natural one. One natural reaction is anger at others, either family members or professionals, who have not been as helpful as they might have been. Because so many people are not well informed about the nature and management of bipolar disorder, such examples will probably not be hard to find. Anger in such a circumstance may well be both natural and justified. But ask yourself: 'Who is this anger really hurting? Is it helping me to make my situation better, or is it holding me back?' Not everyone feels able to do it, but the decision to try to give up one's anger is often an important first step towards change.

As discussed in chapter 5, a useful next step is often to express one's anger, either in speech or writing. A sympathetic listener, either a therapist, family member or friend, can often be very helpful. It is important to give the sufferer space to repeatedly express angry feelings. At first, both sufferer and helper may feel that this hasn't changed anything, but over time angry feelings often do decrease. An alternative approach is to express one's anger in writing, again as discussed in chapter 5. Long angry letters to the person you feel has done you wrong can often, over time, reduce angry feelings. It is probably useful not to send these letters, at least at first, but to work on refining them and making them express your anger and sense of grievance as exactly as possible. You should also give a thought to what possible bad consequences might follow if the letter is sent, and only send it if you are prepared to deal with them.

Should you send such a letter? Alternatively, should you actually speak to the person and tell them how you feel? Of course you have a perfect right to do this, but we caution that this is probably not a step to rush in to. When we feel wronged, we would always like a humble apology from the guilty party, but very often that person either does not feel they have done wrong or will not admit to it. If you do confront the person you feel has let you down, be prepared for any possible answer, and only confront them if you will feel good about doing it whatever the outcome.

Below is an example of how, through therapy, one patient was able to overcome his sense of having been wronged.

case | *Donald spent a considerable amount of time in therapy discussing his past. In particular, he was angry at some of the doctors who had treated him, feeling that if they had handled his case better, he might not have had to leave university. With this went a sense of loss due to his failure to complete university and thus to obtain the good job that a university education might have made possible for him. The therapy did not take away either his anger or his sense of loss, but it did make it possible for him to begin taking courses. An initial barrier to enrolment for Donald was the thought, 'What good will these courses do me? I still won't be able to get a good job.' Fortunately, he was able to put these thoughts to one side and has gained a lot of satisfaction from his course work.*

Guilt

For some, the alternating highs and lows of bipolar disorder can be a source of guilt. Sufferers may remember specific incidents that happened when they were high. When high, a particular piece of behaviour may seem perfectly justified or only a minor embarrassment; the same incident, when the sufferer is low, might seem to be terribly embarrassing, completely wrong or grossly inconsiderate to others. The depressed sufferer may also look back on what seems to be a wasted life filled with missed opportunities and wrong turns, such as in the following example.

case | *Laverne spent much of her time in therapy talking about the fact that she felt her life was a failure. She tended to focus on her lack of professional attainment and the fact that her poorly paid job prevented her from spending more money on her daughter. She was encouraged to discuss these feeling with her daughter, who told her that, hard as their life had been, she was filled with gratitude for the love and care Laverne had shown to her. Cognitive techniques, as discussed in chapters 3 and 4, were used to help her develop a more realistic view of what she had accomplished in her life.*

Sometimes, when you are in a depressed state, guilty thoughts about a past incident can obsess you. The incident may have seemed minor at the time, but now it feels terrible, and you see yourself as a monster of cruelty or selfishness. It may then replay itself in the mind, inducing feelings of guilt and shame. Once again, cognitive techniques can be used to deal with these feelings. It is important to ask yourself, 'Is there any benefit, to myself or anyone else, in these feelings?' A certain amount of guilt over a past event encourages us to behave better in the future, but too much guilt helps no one. Sometimes, a sincere apology to the person you feel you've wronged, either in person or in writing, can be helpful. Another possibility might be an act of restitution, for example giving a sum of money to a worthy charity, although it is probably wise not to do this while one is in either a depressed or a manic state, for fear of regretting the decision later. It can also be helpful to look at all the people who are responsible for the incident: very seldom is a bad event the sole responsibility of a single person. The technique of the 'Responsibility Pie' (see figure 2) can be useful: make a pie chart apportioning blame to yourself and everyone else involved. This exercise can help put one's own guilt in perspective, as in the following example.

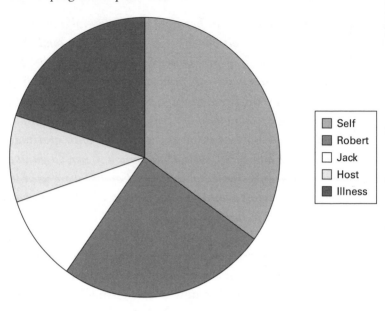

Figure 2 Responsibility Pie

case

A recent low period for Melissa began with an incident at a party. The host had purchased many bottles of fine wine and relatively little food. Melissa felt like dancing while Robert, her husband, seemed reluctant. Melissa began dancing with another guest, a man called Jack, and the two began to flirt with one another. Finally Melissa kissed Jack and, when they got home, a blazing argument with Robert followed. As her mood went down, Melissa began to feel that she had behaved terribly and deserved to lose Robert. Through discussion she came to see that she was not the only one responsible for what had happened. Robert had not really made an effort to enjoy himself at the party or to discuss his feelings with Melissa, Jack had known about Melissa's relationship with Robert but had behaved very seductively, and their host had encouraged everyone to drink as much as possible. Melissa also came to see that her illness had played a role in what had

case

happened, and that she was not responsible for having an illness, though she was responsible for learning how to manage it. Much of this discussion was formulated in terms of a pie chart (see figure 2). This exercise was very helpful to Melissa: she came to see that she hadn't behaved well, but she could learn from her mistakes. She also discussed the incident with Robert, who admitted that he hadn't handled the situation as well as he could have.

Nothing is this chapter is meant to imply that feelings of stigma, loss, anger and guilt are easy to deal with. They can remain ongoing problems for many sufferers. However, all of us can learn, over time, how to manage ourselves and our problems more effectively, and this is true whether you have a long-term illness or not.

POINTS COVERED IN THIS CHAPTER

1. Many members of the public do have incorrect and preju-diced beliefs about mental illness in general and bipolar disorder in particular. However, a mental illness is an illness like any other, and no more of a cause for shame than diabetes or heart disease.

2. Like many other illnesses, bipolar disorder is treatable with a variety of well-established treatments. It almost never makes the sufferer more dangerous than he or she would be anyway.

3. The diagnosis of bipolar disorder, like all psychiatric diag-noses, covers people with a wide variety of symptoms, prob-lems and levels of functioning. Your diagnosis, by itself, tells very little about you, although it may help to guide treatment.

4. Stigma can be dealt with in a variety of ways, including avoiding situations, hiding your problems and trying to educate others about your condition. The best approach is probably a flexible combination of these.

5. Emotions such as anger, a sense of loss, or guilt are all common in sufferers of bipolar disorder, and in fact in many people who suffer from a chronic illness. All these emotions are understandable, but we hope that psychological approaches can help to alleviate their bad effects.

Chapter 11

Survival issues

This chapter concerns practical issues that are of relevance to all of us. People with a diagnosis of bipolar disorder often require medication and psychological treatment to help them manage their illness. However, these individual treatments are rarely sufficient on their own. The many other aspects of the individual's life can have a crucial effect on his or her mental and physical health.

A number of target areas are discussed in this chapter, based on our clinical experience, which indicates that many people with bipolar disorder will have experienced some similar problems. As noted in previous chapters, the way to deal with difficulties of this type is to take a problem-solving approach. This means that rather than blaming yourself or blaming the world for the difficulties you experience, it is often best to sit down and try to evaluate the pros and cons of the things you currently do. If they are causing you or the people you care about significant problems, then a change can be important. If you plan to change in any particular area, it is also important that you don't try to do this all at once. As noted earlier in this book, our experience is that many people with a diagnosis of bipolar disorder are highly motivated and even 'driven' individuals. This can have many significant benefits. However, one of the risks is that such people can tend to set themselves very difficult targets when a decision is made to change. This can be disheartening if such levels of change are not achieved and can put a person off continuing to move forward. If, however, targets are set at a more slow and steady level, substantial progress can be made without the risks of either exhaustion or disappointment and with greater flexibility to cope with those days (which most people experience) when you just find it hard to face 'doing the right thing'. If and when this does happen, don't spend time dwelling on it. The important thing is that you then pick up where you left off the following day. One day or so when things are not on track will not send you back to square one if you then return to using the approaches and ideas discussed.

Money

This can be a significant problem for people with bipolar disorder. Many people with a diagnosis of bipolar disorder manage to hold down regular work, others are able only to work part-time or are not able to obtain or sustain regular employment. This means that money can be tight and that great self-discipline and creativity are needed to avoid falling into debt. The problem is often compounded by additional difficulties caused by spending when unwell. Many people have, whilst in a manic state, spent large sums that they could ill afford. Now that credit is so readily available, people have much more potential to get into levels of debt that are very hard to get out of. This is by no means limited to people with a bipolar diagnosis, but clearly the risks are higher when you might experience a change in mood in which the normal barriers to high spending are taken away by feelings of powerfulness and unrealistic optimism. In addition to high levels of spending, other people may have got into financial trouble in their business lives through investing in risky ventures or ill-advised efforts to expand into new areas.

Most of us find it difficult to face up to mistakes that we have made. When these mistakes are financial and may have an impact not only for you as an individual, but for your family and possibly others, they can be doubly hard to face. Hence, some people will bury their heads in the sand and hope the problem will go away. Of course, the difficulty is that it doesn't and, if ignored, tends to get worse. If you are involved with a mental-health team, then social workers and other team members will be able to provide help and advice on addressing these problems. They will also be able to provide helpful information on whether, if you are receiving benefits, you are actually receiving all that you are entitled to, as many people are not.

Not everyone is involved with this sort of team, however, and you may have a psychiatrist or family doctor as your main clinical contact. In this case, it might be useful to obtain advice on debt management from other experts, such as those in the Citizens' Advice Bureau or elsewhere, who can help develop a financial-management plan. According to the National Depressive and Manic Depressive Association (NDMDA), American nonprofit debt assistance is available from agencies such as Ameridebt and Profina Debt Solutions. Advice on local organisations, which vary from state to state, is best obtained through local community health centres or the state government's department of human services.

For people who have successfully dealt with financial difficulties, there are also the issues of what might happen if they become unwell again. Patients who are currently doing well have often expressed their concern that they might put this all at risk again if their mood were to become high. One preventative approach that has been useful for some people is to make an agreement with another trusted person, usually a spouse or other relative. This agreement would be in the form of a contract, in which the person with bipolar disorder agrees to the other individual (who obviously must be someone whom they trust and who is trustworthy) managing their financial affairs, should their mood become dangerously elevated. Such a document would need to specify, in terms agreed by both parties, how to identify when the individual's mood had changed to a dangerous point and also the extent of financial control that the other individual would have. Other people, such as Melissa in the example below, have taken the simpler path of handing over temptations such as store and credit cards to a partner or returning them to the bank.

case

Melissa encountered financial problems after using her credit cards excessively during a period of elevated mood in her early twenties. She has now paid off most of the debts she ran up, but this has taken a long time. She now avoids the risk of repeating this situation by not having any credit cards at all. She also resists the temptation to obtain store cards. To compensate for the restraint required, she also saves on a regular basis for occasional shopping sprees, which she regards as a form of 'safe thrill'. As she is then using money she can afford to spend, she experiences some of the excitement of previous periods of spending but without the distress of subsequently being unable to meet the bills associated with such sprees.

Housing issues

There used to be a common view that anyone with a serious mental-health problem needed to be held in hospital on a long-term basis. However, these views have thankfully been challenged over the years and now there is a more general acceptance that people with psychiatric disorders, including people with bipolar disorder, can generally live in the same independent way that people who do not happen to have a psychiatric diagnosis do.

One unfortunate effect of previous views of mental-health problems is that people with bipolar disorder can sometimes risk being too independent. This means that sometimes, wishing to avoid admission to hospital or more intensive clinical input, there may a temptation to underplay the impact of life stresses or developing symptoms. The risk this runs is that problems may escalate and lead to the sort of feared outcome that had prompted this behaviour originally, such as a sectioned admission to hospital.

Some of the options that are important to consider are detailed below.

1. *Respite accommodation.* For people who normally live independently, there can be times in which mood is low or unstable when additional help might be useful but when actually being in hospital is not necessary. Recognition of this has led to the development of some respite hostels where people can stay and receive greater support when it is needed, but without the restrictions on independence associated with a stay in hospital. Information on the availability of these resources locally can normally be obtained through local mental-health teams and social services departments. Often, self-help groups (listed in Appendix A) will be able to advise as well.

2. *Supported accommodation.* For some people, the challenge of independent living may prove too difficult at some periods in their lives. Again the use of supported housing, either via local-authority schemes or accessed via mental-health services, can be helpful. Different levels of support can be available from 24-hour staffed hostels to flats with support workers. Levels of provision vary from area to area and again the knowledge of local clinicians and social workers can be useful in finding what is available in your area. State and federal government schemes exist for support/assisted living situations for people with mental illnesses. However, these vary from state to state. Advice on local organisations is best obtained through the individual's local community health centre or state government's department of human services.

3. *Support with independent living.* Developing a support system is important for all of us. To maintain a home, a support system will include an informal network of friends and family but also of people enlisted to help with practical problems. These support systems can be difficult to maintain for people who have had periods of time in hospital or who have moved around after relationship problems. These issues can be important ones to address. Self-help groups and local authorities can provide useful information to help build up a network of support so that independent living does not lead to living in an isolated and lonely situation in which practical problems go unresolved.

Sexual behaviour

Issues associated with sexual behaviour are primarily around difficulties that can arise when mood is high and also the consequences of previous behaviour in periods of elevated mood. Consequences of mania or hypomania can include an increased interest in sexual activity, increased feelings of sensuality, sexualised thoughts, conversation and behaviour. This can lead to engagement in forms of sexual behaviour that, for that person, might otherwise be out of character. The risks associated with mood-dependent changes in sexual behaviour include:

1. Consequences to ongoing, long-term relationships of short-term sexual contacts;
2. Physical risks of unprotected sex;
3. Psychological risks of acting 'out of character'.

The issue here is not a moral one. Some people have a lifestyle that involves more than one partner, or frequent relationship changes. This is not a problem when it is consistent with how the person generally views himself or herself. The problem is when this behaviour puts at risk the style of life a person would normally choose, due to behaviour being directed by a changed mood state, such as in the example below, rather than by the choices he or she would normally make.

case

As noted in chapter 1, there was one occasion when Melissa was in a period of elevated mood that she engaged in an episode of group sex. This was out of character for her and although the men involved had not forced her to take part, they had clearly taken advantage of her vulnerable state. As well as her emotional distress after this incident, Melissa was concerned about her health, in particular risk of AIDS, as the sex had been unprotected. She was finally given the all clear after a blood test, but this was a very difficult and anxious period for her. This type of incident has not happened subsequently but Melissa has noted that when her mood is high she becomes very sociable and extremely flirtatious. This can cause significant strain on her marriage. She has worked on identifying mood changes early on so that she can decide whether or not to put herself in situations where this might be a risk if her mood is elevating. Usually she tends to avoid these situations when she rates her mood as +6 or above. This gives her the flexibility to enjoy being sociable, but not as problematically flirtatious, when her mood is positive but within 'normal' limits.

As noted in chapter 5, an important issue in coping with bipolar disorder is monitoring mood closely to develop a sense of mood changes that are within normal limits and mood changes that are associated with becoming manic or depressed. Practising this sort of mood monitoring, which is best done with the help of a clinician, can help to identify when risky behaviour might become more likely. When early signs of such changes are detected, most people are able to make a choice as to whether to resist such changes by avoiding risky situations or to collude by exposing themselves to further risk. It can sometimes be helpful to have an agreement with a trusted friend or relative that allows that person to indicate when mood changes are reaching a risky level.

Social support and self-help

Social support is important. This can come from family, although this varies from person to person. It can also come from friends and groups with shared interests. The disruptive effects of fluctuating moods can have an impact on social contacts that people have and it can therefore be important to ensure that energy is put into this area when mood is within normal limits. Self-help groups such as the Manic Depressive Fellowship, in Britain, and the National Depressive and Manic Depressive Association (NDMDA), in the United States, can be an important and normalising source of social support. Some people may use self-help intensively, attending regular local groups sometimes in several different adjacent geographical areas. Other people may choose a more hands-off approach, in which self-help organisations are used for information that the individual can then act on independently. Social support may also come from building up hobbies and interests with like-minded individuals who may well have no experience of mood disorders. Often having a combination of resources from professional, family, self-help and recreational areas can lead to the construction of a flexible and supportive social network, which can be used in different ways depending on different needs at different times. Below is an example of how one patient is gradually feeling able to build up a social network for herself.

case | *Laverne was isolated from her family, whom she had had a difficult relationship with. Since having her daughter and working as a night-time cleaner, she has not had many opportunities to make friendships and, when these have developed, she has often felt too low to keep them going.*

case | *Quite recently Laverne has started attending a local self-help group. She was initially very reserved in this new situation, but has found over time that it has become more comfortable. She has met a number of other single parents, both male and female, who have similar difficulties to her own. Although her mood remains low most of the time, having more social contact with others has helped her to feel less hopeless. As a result, she has begun to consider other activities outside the house as her daughter gets older. Currently, she is planning to join a local gym both for the exercise and for another opportunity to meet other people.*

Relating to professionals – active helping

As noted in chapter 3, coping with bipolar disorder effectively will involve working with professionals. This will often include both medical and psychiatric teams, but will also increasingly include contact with clinical psychologists or other trained psychological therapists. This means that often the individual with bipolar disorder is faced with a number of professionals at different times. The old view used to be that 'doctor knows best'. This has thankfully changed, and most clinicians are well aware of the importance of working in partnership with their patients. To do this effectively will often involve an appreciation of each other's relevant areas of expertise. Thus, each individual with bipolar disorder is an expert in his or her experience of the disorder itself, whilst the clinical professionals will have expertise in the application of their clinical skills to the problems identified by the individual. Clearly it is not always the case that all professionals can be approached in this manner, but identifying those who can and working through them can be helpful. In this way, people can become active mangers of their mental health, negotiating medication, social and psychological issues with their clinicians. This gives individuals a significant voice and reduces the risk of feelings of passivity and merely being 'treated', as if this had no direct bearing on the individual experiencing such treatment.

POINTS COVERED IN THIS CHAPTER

1. Set realistic targets for change. If you go off track, don't be put off; try again tomorrow.
2. Money management is important. In particular, managing the risks of access to credit when mood is becoming high.
3. Finding the right balance between support and independence with housing, as in other areas, is important. Some people may require no support; other people may benefit from varying levels of support at different times.
4. Risky sexual behaviour can be an issue in high mood. Awareness of this risk in each person's own experience is important. Catching mood change early is usually the most important means of avoiding this risk.
5. Social-support networks are important. These will, again, be different for different people. For some people, family will be crucial; for other people, more emphasis will be placed on friends or self-help groups.
6. Relationships with professionals are usually part of living with bipolar disorder. Ideally, these should be constructive relationships in which both parties respect each other's areas of knowledge.

Chapter 12

Your rights and how to protect them

This book as a whole embodies a paradox. On the one hand, in writing about bipolar disorder we are suggesting that there is a body of information about the disorder that most people diagnosed with it would find useful. In other words, we are saying that those who suffer from bipolar disorder have a good deal in common. On the other hand, we have taken pains to emphasise how varied the effects of bipolar disorder are, and how one cannot assume that sufferers are alike. Sufferers vary in severity of illness, course of illness, symptoms, level of functioning, types of medication that are helpful, and so on. It would be perfectly possible to find two sufferers, both with clearly diagnosable cases of bipolar disorder, who have none of these factors in common. The obvious point here is that every sufferer is a unique individual, to be judged according to his or her own character, talents and accomplishments.

At the same time, as we discussed in chapter 10, there are many people who hold a stigmatising view of mental illnesses such as bipolar disorder. Rather than judging you as a person, based on what you are like and what you can do, such people may assume that a diagnosis of bipolar disorder means that you are not capable of making your own decisions or managing your own life. Similarly, they may assume that you are not capable of working, handling money, driving a car, or dealing with life and its problems. It is also fair to say that, at times, many people with bipolar disorder are not capable of some or all of these things. At such times, they may well need to be protected or taken care of. But the key point is that this applies to some sufferers at some times, not all sufferers at all times. When dealing with such people, you should be aware of your rights and of the steps you may need to take to protect them, and that is the subject of this chapter.

The Mental Health Act

The following discussion is based on British law, which is known best. American laws vary from state to state, but the same broad principles apply. As discussed in chapter 3, the Mental Health Act sets forth very strict criteria as to at what times patients can be deprived of their rights by being detained in hospital and treated against their will. To be detained, a patient has to be suffering from a mental illness, a danger to self or others, and refusing treatment. Three professionals – two doctors, one of whom is generally not an employee of the hospital, and a social worker – must agree on these points. Periods of detention are fixed: generally, patients can be detained for twenty-eight days for assessment or six months if doctors believe that they need treatment. This does not mean that patients have to stay for six months, as they can be discharged earlier if their treating team feels they are better. However, it does mean that if the staff feel they need to stay for more than six months, they have to reapply and repeat the process of consulting with an outside doctor.

Under the law, detained patients must have their rights under the Mental Health Act fully explained to them, and they have the right to written information about their conditions of detention. If you are detained, you can also ask for a Mental Health Act worker to meet with you and explain your legal rights. Further, patients have a right of appeal against detention, both to the managers of the hospital and to the Mental Health Act Commission, whose address you will find in the Appendix A of this book. Both the managers and commissioners organise hearings at which detained patients can plead their case. At such hearings, patients also receive free legal representation from solicitors paid by Legal Aid. The Mental Health Act commissioners oversee the administration of the act and take their responsibility to protect the rights of patients very seriously. We have known of a number of cases in our own clinical practice in which patients have been released from detention following a hearing. Commissioners will also periodically visit hospitals, review all paperwork concerning the administration of the Mental Health Act and speak to any patients who have complaints about how they have been treated. In the United States, the system varies from state to state, but in many states lawyers are available through the hospital, and these lawyers are able to seek judicial review for detained patients.

Relatives can have a very important role to play in caring for those suffering from mental illness, and medical teams will often consult with relatives, invite them to meetings and involve them in planning a patient's care. This is recognised in the Mental Health Act, in which the staff are obliged to consult with the 'nearest living relative', a person defined by the act. The person selected in the first instance will be a husband or wife, but this can include long-term partners, even when the couple are not married or are homosexual partners. If there is no partner, the role falls on the oldest child, followed by parents and then brothers and sisters. The mental-health team must consult with the nearest living relative, and cannot detain the patient over a long term without the consent of this person. If the mental-health team feels that the nearest living relative is acting against the patient's best interests, it is possible for that person to be legally 'set aside', but this is quite a lengthy procedure. So, clearly, if you have ever been involuntarily detained or might be in the future, it would be very useful to discuss your situation with your nearest living relative and make your wishes clear to him or her.

The subject of involuntary detention is an upsetting one. To be involuntarily detained can be seen as an insult, as being told 'You can't take care of yourself', or 'You need to be treated like a child.' But there are times, perhaps as a result of an illness or injury, when all of us may need to rely on others to take care of us. If you have been detained, you may well feel that it was not necessary, or that those who detained you did not take account of your wishes. But please bear in mind that the situation is bound to be a difficult one, and that, in general, both professionals and family members will do their best to see that you receive good care. And if the experience of involuntary treatment was unpleasant, all the more reason to try to ensure that you will remain well and not have to undergo it again.

If you have any complaints regarding your treatment while in hospital, or the aftercare you receive, note that all hospitals have systems for handling complaints. It is your right to complain, whether you care was voluntary or involuntary. The right to make a complaint extends to relatives, and even to visitors, who can complain on the patient's behalf. Some complaints may be very useful to the hospital, showing them some flaw in their services. But in any case, you have a right to receive both good treatment and respect, and you should complain if you feel you did not.

Advocacy and support

When you are in hospital, either as a voluntary or a detained patient, meetings with professionals can often feel very stressful. Even a one-on-one meeting with a doctor can provoke a lot of anxiety if you feel that doctor might be making decisions that could have a big influence on your life. Stress and anxiety can grow even worse if you are invited to a large meeting. For example, on many wards there are meetings called 'ward rounds', in which the consultant psychiatrist discusses the care of his or her patients with the whole multi-disciplinary team, sometimes including trainee doctors or nurses. You may be asked to attend these meetings and may face a room with ten or more professionals, many of them people you have not seen before. Similarly, if you are receiving long-term care in the community, you may be asked to attend meetings to review your care. There is no obligation to attend, but it may well be advisable to do so, as this gives you more say in the care you are receiving.

In such situations, you may wish to be accompanied at the hearing by a family member, friend or advocate. Many hospitals have advocacy services, often staffed by trained volunteers, many of whom are themselves mental-health-service users. Many patients have found these advocates to be very helpful, but it is also important to bear in mind that there is no formal obligation to use an advocate if you would prefer a friend or family member, as you are generally entitled to receive help and support from whomever you choose when dealing with professionals. Patient Advocates are also available in many American hospitals. In any case, you may find it helpful to have someone to support you when dealing with doctors or other professionals in any number of circumstances.

There is a variety of situations in which help, support and advice can be invaluable. For example, a manic or depressive episode can lead to financial problems and debts, either through overspending or being unable to work. Such debts might lead to your electricity or telephone being cut off or to rent arrears and housing problems. Similarly, if your illness is severe and disabling, you may need to apply for various forms of benefit and social security. Friends, family or an advocate might be helpful, but there are other sources of help and support. As noted in chapter 3, many hospitals employ benefits advisors, while your care co-ordinator or social worker might be able to offer help or advice. Many hospitals also have access to volunteer 'befriending' services, and many befrienders can provide help and support. If you do not have access to such professionals, your doctor may be able to advise you on how to go about getting it. We can also recommend your local Citizens' Advice Bureau (see Appendix A of this book for the address of their Head Office); this British organisation has done much good work through the years helping people in all sorts of trouble and has what some people see as an added advantage in not being part of the mental-health system. We do not know of an American equivalent, although many of the websites mentioned in Appendix 1 can be very helpful. Another source of help can be found in self-help groups, which we discuss below. The key point is: if you are facing a difficult situation, one in which you are not sure how to proceed, look for advice and help. There is a lot of help available if you go looking for it.

Disability and discrimination

When most people hear the term 'disability', they generally think of a visible physical disability, of someone in a wheelchair or a blind person with a white cane. The term also includes long-term illnesses that are not 'visible', such as asthma or diabetes. However, serious mental illnesses – that is, mental illnesses that are long-term, require ongoing treatment and are unlikely to go away by themselves or be cured – are also considered to be disabilities. Thus, most people with bipolar disorder can be considered to be disabled, a fact that has legal implications for employment and services.

In Britain, under the 1995 Disability Discrimination Act, employers and those providing services to the public must make 'reasonable adjustments' to their conditions of work or service to take account of the needs of those with disabilities. This is especially pertinent in the area of employment. Currently, these rules only apply to firms with fifteen or more employees, but in 2004 this limit will be removed and all firms will be covered. What this means is that if a firm knows that an employee suffers with a disability, it has a duty of care to that employee to take account of this. For example, if you as an employee needed time off to attend appointments with a psychiatrist or psychologist, your employer would be legally obliged to agree as long as the loss of productivity involved was 'reasonable'. Similarly, if a change in office organisation or routine could make your work less stressful, and this change would not result in an 'unreasonable' burden for the employer, the Act would say that your employer should make this change. Obviously there can be disagreement about what is reasonable. If you think that there is a way in which your employers can help you by changing your conditions of working, you can either discuss it with them directly or seek advice. A solicitor who knows about employment law could advise you, and self-help groups, such as the Manic Depression Fellowship, are also good sources of advice. Of course, your employers cannot be expected to make such 'reasonable adjustments' if they do not know about your problem. In the United States, the Americans with Disabilities Act has very similar provisions.

What if you are seeking employment? Again, the Act makes it illegal to discriminate against someone solely because they have a disability. None the less, those with any form of mental illness may worry that disclosing this fact may create a subtle prejudice that can turn the balance in a job application. They may be tempted to conceal their disabilities, but there is an alternative approach. If you are applying for a job, you should feel that the job is within your capabilities and that your illness will not interfere with your ability to do that job successfully. If you are under psychiatric care and receiving medication, you are in a position to explain that these factors will help you to stay stable and do your job successfully. A study carried out by the United Kingdom Department of Health shows that people with bipolar disorder do not have a worse health record than members of the general public. Those who take account of their illness and problems should clearly represent a better prospect for employers than those who do not. The choice is yours, but it is also worth noting that if employers are not told about an employee's disability, they are under no obligation to take account of it.

Driving

Under British law, those suffering from an illness that might impair their ability to drive must notify the Driver and Vehicle Licensing Agency (DVLA); the same applies in most American States, and sufferers should contact their state Motor Vehicle Department. The law covers a variety of physical illnesses, such as diabetes and epilepsy, but also mental illnesses. The literature available from the DVLA, both in print and on their website, states that minor mental-health problems, 'uncomplicated by significant memory or concentration problems, agitation, behavioural disturbance or suicidal thoughts', do not require notification of the DVLA. However, more serious problems, such as episodes of mania, do: 'DVLA must be notified and driving should cease pending the outcome of medical enquiry.' What the DVLA is looking for is confirmation that the driver realises the nature of his or her problem, is taking appropriate medication and is stable for a reasonable period of time, which will vary depending on how ill the driver has been. Documents from a physician or psychiatrist are required to confirm these facts. This may seem onerous, but the DVLA applies the same sorts of restrictions to bipolar disorder as to various physical disorders. The goal is to make driving safer for all, and this has to be a good thing. It is also worth noting that if you have failed to notify the DVLA and get into an accident, the consequences could be very serious. Similarly, American drivers should ensure that they are familiar with the law in their state.

Self-help groups

One organisation with which we have had a fair amount of contact is the British Manic Depression Fellowship. This self-help group offers a variety of services to its members, from advice on self-management and employment to a travel insurance scheme specifically devised for people with bipolar disorder. In our experience, these services can be very valuable specifically because they are based on the experiences of individual people. Further, the chance to meet other people with your problem, to share experiences and feel less different from everyone else can be a tremendously liberating experience. That being said, different self-help groups and different chapters within those groups will vary based on the individuals involved. A group that is extremely important for one person may not be to another's taste. However, in the back of this book we include a list on self-help organisations of various sorts (in the UK, the US, Canada and Australia) with the hope that individual readers will look into them and perhaps find one that is to their taste. The experience of individual support, whether of friends, family, professionals or fellow sufferers, is extremely important for all of us.

POINTS COVERED IN THIS CHAPTER

1. Under current mental health laws, sufferers from mental illnesses can be detained in hospital, but these laws place strict limits on the power to do this. If you feel your rights have been violated, there are several avenues through which you can appeal.
2. The nearest living relative plays a very important role under mental health law and has considerable influence on the way detained patients are treated.
3. A variety of advocates, befrienders, and advisors are available to those who suffer from mental illness.
4. Long-term mental illness is covered by disability discrimination laws, giving employees with disabilities many rights in their places of work.

5. Bipolar disorder can lead to the suspension of one's driving licence, but with medical support, sufferers can get their licences back and drive freely.

6. Many people find self-help groups an important form of support and advice.

A final note

We have written this book primarily for people with bipolar disorder, and secondarily for their families. We hope we have not appeared to minimise the sufferings and difficulties that this disorder has caused for a large number of people. Our message, based on our own experience as clinicians, is one of hope. In most cases, bipolar disorder can be controlled, and people can live happy and fulfilled lives in spite of it. This may require various forms of medical and psychological treatment and social support, but most of all it requires self-acceptance by the person with the disorder and help from friends and family. Having bipolar disorder, or any other illness, does not diminish your value as a person, it simply means that you have a different set of problems to cope with from many other people. If this book can help you to cope a little better, we will be very pleased.

Useful addresses and further reading

Useful addresses

General information

Mental Health Act Commission
Maid Marion House
56 Houndsgate
Nottingham NG1 6BG
Tel: 0115 943 7100
Internet: www.mhac.trent.nhs.uk

National Association of Citizens Advice Bureau
Central Office
Myddelton House
115–123 Pentonville Road
London N1 9LZ
Tel: 020 7833 2181
Internet: www.nacab.org.uk

Self-help organisations

BRITAIN

Depression Alliance
35 Westminster Bridge Road
London SE1 7JB
Tel: 020 7633 0557
Fax: 020 7633 0559

Manic Depressive Fellowship: National Office
Castleworks
21 St George's Road
London SE1 6ES
Tel: 020 7793 2600
Email: mdf@mdf.org.uk

Mental Health Foundation: UK Office
20–21 Cornwall Terrace
London NW1 4QL
Tel: 020 7535 7400
Email: mhf@mentalhealth.org.uk

MIND (The National Association for Mental Health)
15–19 Broadway
London E15 4BQ
Tel: 020 8519 2122
Fax: 020 8522 1725
Email: contact@mind.org.uk

Mood Swings Network
23 Mount Street
Manchester M4 4DE
Tel: 0161 953 4105

USA AND CANADA

Canadian Mental Health Association
2160 Yonge, 3rd Floor
Toronto
ON MAS 2Z3
Canada
Tel: 416 484 7750
Email: national@cmha.ca

Depression and Related Affective Disorders Association
(DRADA)
Meyer 3–181, 600 North Wolfe Street
Baltimore
MD 21287–7381
USA
Tel: 410 955 4647
Email: drada@jhmi.edu

Mood Disorders Society of Canada
Ste. 266, 35–2855
Pembina Hwy
Winnipeg
Manitoba
Canada
Tel: 204 475 3531
Email: washdown@mb.sympatico.ca

National Alliance for the Mentally Ill (NAMI)
Colonial Place Three
2107 Wilson Blvd, Suite 300
Arlington
VA 22201
USA
Tel: 703 524 7600
Helpline: 1800 950 NAMI [6264]

National Depressive and Manic-Depressive Association
730 N. Franklin Street, Suite 501
Chicago
Illinois 60610–7204
USA
Tel: 800 826 3632 or
312 642 0049
Fax: 312 642 7243
Email: info@ndmda.org

AUSTRALIA

Depression and Mood Disorders Association of New South Wales
Friendship House
60 Victoria Road
Gladesville
New South Wales
Australia
Tel: Mental Health Information Service 02 9816 5688 (free call 1800 674 200)

Mindcare Limited
Friendship House
20 Balfour Street
New Farm 4005
Queensland
Australia
Tel: 07 358 4988

Self-help on the web

Below are listed just a few of the many available sites on the internet relating to bipolar disorder.

www.bipolarworld.net

An American information and support site for people with bipolar disorder, run mainly by service users. Includes chat rooms and internet-search services for bipolar-related topics.

www.depressionalliance.org

The site for the depression alliance (address above), which provides information on UK self-help groups as well as email contacts and chat rooms on bipolar disorder and depression more generally.

www.mcmanweb.com

An American site run by someone with a diagnosis of bipolar disorder, who previously worked as a financial journalist. It provides information and updates on clinical research into bipolar disorder, as well as input from other service users and a discussion forum.

www.mdf.org.uk

A British site for the Manic Depressive Fellowship (address above), which provides information on local self-help groups in the UK, contact information for MDF and listings of current MDF publications.

www.mentalhealth.org.uk

This Mental Health Foundation website covers mental-health issues relating to children and adults. It also funds research into these areas, and provides information on this. A number of the initiatives being developed by the Mental Health Foundation are described here, including their development of services with a significant amount of user involvement.

www.mind.org.uk

The British site for MIND (address above). A broad-ranging site covering self-help information, information on local MIND groups and email contacts. This site also provides information on current MIND campaigns and projects and opportunities within the organisation for voluntary and paid employment.

www.ndmda.org

An American site, providing educational information and support for people with bipolar disorder and depression.

www.pendulum.org

Another American site, providing information on recent developments in bipolar disorder. Books relevant to bipolar disorder are listed and recent, usually American, research is highlighted. Informal jokes- and fun-pages are included. The site has a bipolar-focused search engine.

www.windsofchange.com

A Canadian site, providing information on topics relevant to people with bipolar disorder and their carers. Again, there is a forum on the site for users and carers.

Further reading

Berger, D., Berger, I., Bergem, D. and Vuckovic, A. 1992. *We Heard the Angels of Madness: A Family Guide to Coping With Manic Depression.* London, Quill (Harper)

Copeland, M. E. 1994. *Living Without Depression and Manic Depression: A Workbook for Maintaining Mood Stability.* Oakland, New Harbinger

Court B. L. and Nelson, G. E. 1996. *Bipolar Puzzle Solution: A Mental Health Client's Perspective.* New York, Accelerated Development

Fawcett. J, Golden, B., Rosenfelf, N. and Goodwin, F. K. 2000. *New Hope for People With Bipolar Disorder.* Roseville, Prima Publishing

Jamison, K. R. 1997. *An Unquiet Mind.* New York, Picador

McKeon, P. 1995. *Coping With Depression and Elation.* London, Sheldon

Mondimore, F. M. 1999. *Bipolar Disorder: A Guide for Patients and Families.* Baltimore, Johns Hopkins Press Health Book

Worthen, M. 2001. *Journey Not Chosen. Destination Not Known: Living With Bipolar Disorder.* Little Rock, August House Publishers

References cited in chapter 4

Goodwin, F. K. and Jamison K. R. 1990. *Manic-Depressive Illness*. New York, Oxford University Press

Lam, D., Bright, J., Jones, S., Hayward, P., Schuck, N., Chisholm, D. and Sham, P. 2000. 'Cognitive therapy for bipolar illness – a pilot study of relapse prevention', *Cognitive Therapy & Research*, 24: 503–520.

Lam, D. H., Watkins, E. R., *et al*. 2003. 'A randomized controlled study of cognitive therapy for relapse prevention for bipolar affective disorder: outcome of the first year', *Archives of General Psychiatry*, 60: 145–52.

Scott, J., Garland, A. and Moorhead, S. 2001. 'A pilot study of cognitive therapy in bipolar disorders', *Psychological Medicine* 31, 459–67.

Appendix B

Deep muscle relaxation

This appendix describes deep muscle relaxation, a technique that is often used by clinical psychologists. If you wish to use it, you need a comfortable chair and a quiet room. You can record these words onto an audiotape or ask a friend with a soothing voice to do it for you. The person recording should speak in a slow, calming tone, and can repeat parts of the tape several times in a relaxing manner if you find this helpful. Relaxation is a skill; if you find that the tape is not that relaxing at first, we suggest that you practise it several times. The goal is to pay attention to the feelings of tension and relaxation in the varying muscle groups and gradually learn how relaxation feels, which can then help you learn how to make your muscles more and more relaxed. Finally, we provide a tranquil scene for you to visualise at the end of the tape, but if you don't like it, you can imagine and describe another one that you personally find most relaxing. Now follows the relaxation technique.

I'd like you to close your eyes, sit comfortably, and relax. If there's any tension anywhere in your body, just let it relax away. Your body should be very loose and limp and relaxed, very loose and limp and relaxed, just relax. Good. Now I'd like you to tense your right hand. Just make a fist with your right hand. I'd like you to feel all the feelings of tension in your right hand. Just feel how that feels. Good. Now, relax, relax. Just let your right hand relax. Just feel the feelings of relaxation in your right hand. Just feel how that feels. Your right hand is very loose, and limp, and relaxed. Good.

Now I'd like you to tense your left hand. Just make a fist with your left hand. I'd like you to feel all the feelings of tension in your left hand. Just feel how that feels. Good! Now, relax, relax. Just let your left hand relax. Just feel the feelings of relaxation in your left hand. Just feel how that feels. Your left hand is very loose, and limp, and relaxed. Good.

Now I'd like you to tense up your right upper arm. You can do this by touching your right shoulder with your right hand and making your arm very tense. Try to feel all the feelings of tension in your right arm. Try to feel how that feels. Now, relax, relax. Just let your right arm relax. Just feel the feelings of relaxation in your right arm. Just feel how that feels. Your right arm and right hand are very loose, and limp, and relaxed, very loose and limp and relaxed. Good.

Now I'd like you to tense up your left upper arm. You can do this by touching your left shoulder with your left hand and making your arm very tense. Try to feel all the feelings of tension in you left arm. Try to feel how that feels. Now, relax, relax. Just let your left arm relax. Just feel the feelings of relaxation in your left arm. Just feel how that feels. Your left arm and left hand are very loose, and limp, and relaxed, very loose and limp and relaxed. Good.

Now I'd like you to tense up your shoulders. Shrug up your shoulders towards your ears. Your shoulders are very tense, try to feel all the feelings of tension in your shoulders. Try to feel how that feels. Good. Now, relax, relax. Just let your shoulders relax. Your shoulders should be very loose and limp and relaxed, very loose and limp and relaxed, your shoulders and arms should be very loose and limp and relaxed. Good.

Now I'd like you to relax your neck. Just gently let your head roll from side to side. Don't do this too vigorously, but just gently rotate your neck back and forth and let all those muscles relax. Just let your whole upper body relax. You should feel very loose and limp and relaxed. Good.

Now take a deep breath. Hold it (pause about 1 second) and now let it out. And as you let it out, you feel all the tension leaving your body. You feel very loose and limp and relaxed. Good.

Now tense up your right foot. You can do this by curling up your toes. Just feel all the tension in your right foot. Try to feel how that feels. And now, relax, relax. Just let your right foot relax. Your right foot should be very loose and limp and relaxed. Very loose and limp and relaxed. Try to feel how that feels. Good.

Now tense up your left foot. You can do this by curling up your toes. Just feel all the tension in your left foot. Try to feel how that feels. And now, relax, relax. Just let your left foot relax. Your left foot should be very loose and limp and relaxed. Very loose and limp and relaxed. Try to feel how that feels. Good.

Now tense up your right leg. Just press down hard with your right heel and tense up your right leg. Try to feel all the tension in you right leg. Try to feel how that feels. And now, relax. Just let your right leg relax. Your right leg and your right foot should be very loose and limp and relaxed. Very loose and limp and relaxed. Try to feel how that feels. Good.

Now tense up your left leg. Just press down hard with your left heel and tense up your left leg. Try to feel all the tension in you left leg. Try to feel how that feels. And now, relax. Just let your left leg relax. Your left leg and your left foot should be very loose and limp and relaxed. Both your legs and both your feet should be very loose and limp and relaxed. Try to feel how that feels. Good.

Now tense up your stomach. Tighten up all the muscles in your stomach. Try to feel all the tension in your stomach, try to feel how that feels. Now, relax, relax. Just let your stomach relax. Your stomach should be very loose and limp and relaxed.

Your whole lower body should be very loose and limp and relaxed. Try to feel all the feelings of relaxation in your lower body, try to feel how that feels. Good.

Now take a deep breath. Hold it (pause about 1 second) and now let it out. And as you let it out, you feel all the tension leaving your body. You feel very loose and limp and relaxed. Good.

Now tense up all the muscles of your forehead. Just wrinkle up your forehead, try to feel all the tension in your forehead, try to feel how that feels. And now, relax, relax. Just let your forehead relax. Your forehead should be very loose and limp and relaxed, very loose and limp and relaxed. Good.

Now tense up your eyes. Squeeze your eyes tight shut, try to feel all the tension in your eyes. And now, relax, relax. Just let your eyes relax. Your eyes should feel very loose and limp and relaxed, very loose and limp and relaxed. Try to feel how that feels. Good.

Now tense up your nose. Wrinkle up your nose, try to feel all the tension in your nose. And now, relax, relax. Just let your nose relax. Your nose should feel very loose and limp and relaxed, very loose and limp and relaxed. Try to feel how that feels. Good.

Now tense up your cheeks. Pull back your cheeks in a wide grin, try to feel all the tension in your cheeks. And now, relax, relax. Just let your cheeks relax. Your cheeks should feel very loose and limp and relaxed, very loose and limp and relaxed. Try to feel how that feels. Good.

Now finally, tense up your jaw. Clench your teeth, and try to feel all the tension in your jaw. And now, relax, relax. Just let your jaw relax. Your jaw should feel very loose and limp and relaxed, very loose and limp and relaxed. Try to feel how that feels. Good.

Now take a deep breath. Hold it (pause about 1 second) and now let it out. And as you let it out, you feel all the tension leaving your body. You feel very loose and limp and relaxed. Good.

Now I'm going to count from one to five, and as I do, you're going to feel more and more relaxed. If there's any tension anywhere in your body, just let it relax away. One. Relax, relax. Two. You feel very loose and limp and relaxed, very loose and limp and relaxed. Three. Just let all the tension leave your body. Four. Relax, relax. You feel very loose and limp and relaxed. Five.

Now you feel very relaxed and very comfortable. If there's any tension anywhere in your body, just let it relax away. It's just as if you were lying on a beautiful sandy beech. You feel very relaxed and you haven't a care in the world. You're lying on a beautiful sandy beach, and the warm sun is beating down on you, and you feel very comfortable. Far away you can hear the surf, and you can hear the seagulls crying and children playing on the beach and some music on a transistor radio, but it's all very far away. A gentle breeze is blowing, so you don't feel hot, just very warm and pleasant. When you open your eyes you see beautiful fluffy clouds floating in the blue sky, and the ocean is in front of you, with a gentle swell and a few boats in the distance. You lie back and close your eyes, and you feel very relaxed and very at peace. You haven't a care in the world. You feel a deep sense of peace and contentment. Now you can relax for as long as you want to, just enjoying this feeling of total relaxation. And when you are ready, you can slowly open your eyes and wake up.

Index

Page numbers in **bold** represent figures or tables